Once a Week Strategy to Stop Procrastination

The Practical Step-by-Step Guide to Doing Difficult Things, Ignoring Distractions, Improving Productivity, and Overcoming Procrastination for Good

BRAD MEIER

ISBN 978-9-69-239234-1

9 789692 392341 >

Table of Contents

Preface

Procrastination is very common. It is a major problem most people have to live or deal with. It has eaten deep into many lives and created more problems than we can ever imagine. Procrastination is a source of many evil or dangers that many face today. Many people have tried to deal with it. They've tried all their best possible to overcome it, but all to no avail. It has become a pain in the neck for some people, many have done different things and followed different rules just to make it stop, to be free from it, as it has become like an addiction that has refused to leave, but they find themselves in its pit at the end of the day.

This book is very important. It is an essential tool that one should not be without. I see it as something that will keep me going and help me achieve my aims and goals and objectives without much stress or burden, or difficulty. Since the beginning of the age, procrastination has been something that man has had to deal with one way or the other. And it has eaten deep into the potential and future of many, whether they are aware of it or not. That's why this book has been provided for everyone to be aware of what procrastination really is, the dangers of procrastination, and how to fight it, how to overcome it, how to get it eliminated before it eliminates one's life and purpose.

One of the major things in this book is the concept of awareness, motivation, and action. It is being aware of what procrastination is, the dangers it breeds, and many more about it that get you motivated to do the right thing, give it all it takes to stop it, and even help others be free from it. It is the awareness of the truth that makes you want to act on the truth. When there is no awareness, there is never going to be moving forward. Awareness is the state, level, or quality of being conscious of a thing or situation.

Motivation comes from awareness. It is the willingness to action, an incentive, or a reason for doing something. So what happens when there is motivation? Motivation prompts you to act. It is what makes you feel like doing something. It is that desire in you to do something, to take a step or action. After knowing about procrastination, it is the motivation that makes you want to do things that will end it. It will make you want to follow the once-a-week plan. Motivation is said to be the engine of action. That is, without the former, action can never take place. It is motivation that pushes action into life or reality.

So what does action do? It creates in you a new awareness, and that's one it continues. That new awareness is created in you again, another motivation to do something new or different, better than the former one; then you take another action, and so on. Before you know it, you become someone totally different from who you have always been. Taking action makes you different. It improves your person, your personality. When you get motivated to take an action that will help you eliminate procrastination and make you a better person, and you take it, be sure to get another awareness of yourself. You know yourself as a different person. And that will get you motivated to do something again. All these bring out the potential in you and build you into the great person you were meant to be.

But why does it seem impossible for the above to take place? Distraction is a major factor. Things that get one's attention divided. We find it difficult to concentrate, so we resolve to ping things that are not relevant, giving up important things, things we ought to do to mundane things. But the eyes of many are blind to the fact that distractions are like drugs that give you immediate or present satisfaction. They make you happy and fulfilled in the present. But builds a strong foundation of damaged future and ambition. In other words, distractions keep your eyes and mind off the important things you are supposed to do or engage in and give you pleasure in the present. But unknowingly, makes you destroy your future and potential. So we have to block distractions as much as we can by working on the things that distract us and doing away with them.

Another thing we've found out that works is eliminating choices. When there are many choices, there is this motion of '*missed opportunities*' it creates, which in turn causes depression and makes you feel like a failure. That compared to the many opportunities we have, every choice we make will be sub-optimal. When there are too many choices, we won't get the right satisfaction we ought to get from the decisions we make, even if they become a success.

What do we have to do then? We have to get them eliminated. This means we have to create a context in which the only options required or available are the ones that will be useful for achieving our aims or goals and objectives. This helps us take the bull of procrastination by its horns, live by our own rules, and then fulfill our purpose.

Also, making difficult things easy. One major reason many people procrastinate is not having a clue where to start. There is this fear of not being up to par, of not being successful, of being faced with something that is difficult to do and drains energy. What is needed? A Work Breakdown Structure which will be expatiated more in the book. It is also known as WBS. It is nothing more than a detailed list of all the activities involved in a project; it's like a shopping list. It is created with the goal of reducing an articulated and complex project to its minimum terms, getting its elementary activities recognized. All that has to be done is to get hold of your project and start dismantling it one brick after the other until the basic activities are recognized or identified. But above all, the first activity to be performed. The ability to start with the simplest activity is the real move of winning.

In my experience, if there will be anything like a self-respecting change, it is a necessity that it translates into an everyday habit. This allows us to achieve our goals and objectives with the auto-pilot on. The same thing applies to the fight against procrastination. If we are to win this battle, if we won't end up becoming a slave to procrastination, we must lay a strong foundation of anti-postponed habits in our lives. I have suggested many of the habits. They will help you define a simple, clear, concise lineup for real change. In this book, you have all the tools and weapons to fight and win, to overcome and climb the mountains you thought were impossible to climb. This OaW method can change you as a person and not just overcome procrastination. It is a method of facing life problems, or life generally, not just a cure to procrastination.

Not only will this book help to put an end to procrastination, but it also has a way of making you a better person in the nearest future as you follow the guide obediently and consistently. It helps you create habits that will not only help you to achieve your goals at the right time but will also make you busy with the right things, things that will build you into a better person, a great person in the nearest future. There's this excitement that comes with knowing you have a once-a-week plan you are following. There's this joy it breeds in you to know you are going to do a new thing tomorrow. This book is going to help you with that, and you will even lend the book to someone else that needs it.

But one important thing you should note and that should always be on your mind as you read through this book is that you can read only the theory but not the practice. This is because you yourself are the practice. You have to do it yourself; you have to take action. Without that, the knowledge you acquire will just be wasted in your mind.

This OaW plan is written to provide you with immediately applicable and clearly effective advice. But even the world's best advice is not sufficient sometimes to achieve those goals we wish for. For certain techniques to be effective, they must be experienced within a path. Practice is the concept of getting well.

INTRODUCTION

If today we do not live the life we want, it is because yesterday we decided to postpone it until tomorrow.

Procrastination comes from the Latin word procrastinàre, composed of "pro" ("forward") and "cràstinus" ("to tomorrow"); then procrastinate means literally "postpone to tomorrow."

Can you recall when you planned a task for the next day and then forwarded it again to the next? Postponing until tomorrow? How many times have you done it? Even on crucial examinations, you still shift your preparation to the following minutes, hours, or days. The greatest truth about the whole thing is that you never postpone fun stuff.

When you feel like playing video games, you just do it. Time to eat, sleep, or watch your favourite show never gets postponed. But challenging tasks like dieting, hitting the gym, stopping a habit, or learning a skill suffers your inability to just get it started. They are always the task for the next day.

I guess I got very close, right? For many of us, "putting off until tomorrow" is a way of life. No matter how hard we try to be productive and meet our goals. We can still not force ourselves to do what we want to do. Tomorrow always seems like the best day to have time for everything, and that tomorrow never comes because you still need a tomorrow to get it done every day. Deep down, you know the importance of these things you postpone and often beat yourself about it. You feel terrible when you realize that the day was far spent, and you still have these tasks undone. If all of these describe you, you are a *procrastinator*, and this book is your last stop to putting off until tomorrow.

Procrastination, in one way or another, underlies all our failures, missed goals, and lack of fulfilment. In this book, you will find the most effective techniques to free yourself from procrastination permanently. But all these will only work if you are willing to take action. Only actions will change your life; ideas never will. Unfortunately, this is a reality we love to ignore. Ideas, programs, resolutions, and plans do not exist; rather, they exist but do not change the world. After all, how can something that is only inside our brain lead to fundamental changes? Telekinesis is a fantastic superpower, but, I'll tell you a secret, we humans do not have it.

Changing the world requires actions like talking to others, doing or avoiding doing certain things, moving from one place to another, writing this, and saying that. You must do something to achieve your desired result. So, this book is well packed with a proven strategy to help you overcome procrastination problems. And I call it proven because I have been in your shoes before, which helps me. All techniques discussed here will only work if you act on them. Be prepared to practice all that is advised. Everything is yet another theory until you set yourself to be practical and exhibit all theories in reality. That practice has to be now.

The community of personal development or self-help is full of theories that can help you solve your problem. The help is not in theory itself but in how you let these theories influence your activities in reality. Back then, I mainly focused on buying any best-selling book, reading them, and expecting the theories to play into my problems and solve them. Of course, it ended up a complete waste of time until I learned to put the theories into practice.

Don't get too carried away. Relate even facts you read to yourself and them to create a checklist of how the theories discussed will play in your reality. You can get a friend who has similar issues and share your progress. This way, you can keep track of your actions and success. You can make the techniques a competition and see yourself improve by the day. If you are cooking up excuses in your head, like *I don't think I have time for this, I will just read and practice,* Stop it! Yeah, Stop doing that. You can do this, and you must start the action immediately.

This guide is written with the intent to provide you with applicable and practical advice that will help you stop procrastination for good. But sometimes, even the best advice is not enough to achieve the changes we need. So specific techniques must be experienced on this path to freedom. And there are distinct phases of this growth:

- Awareness
- Motivation
- Action

These phases have been explained In full detail in every chapter. They are closely related, and making them follow the correct sequence will help you understand the significance and importance of each phase. It will also help to trigger a circle of virtuous self-generation. Let's begin.

Chapter 1

Awareness generates motivation. Motivation is the engine of Action. Action creates a new awareness in you.

First, I have been a procrastinator, and trust me, dealing with this habit is not an easy thing, but it is not unbreakable. I know you have lots of confusion and misconceptions on your mind now. With research and experience, you will be able to map out your condition and find the best approach to dealing with your procrastinating problem.

Think of this situation as a huge blocker you are trying to push and know that being a procrastinator doesn't make you a complete failure or a lost course. Throughout history, there have been several stories of past leaders, philosophers and people we can count as great men who have procrastinated at one point in their lives. Even if they were famous and had lots of expectations set before them, they still put off their tasks till tomorrow. If you find yourself looking through the window, watching videos on TikTok, or responding to emails and chats instead of completing your task, you are not the only one who has experienced that. Let's go back in history. You might find one famous past person that has a similar situation as yours.

First, Tenzin Gyatso, the 14th Dalai Lama, was a great and well-recognized spiritual leader. He fought for the Tibetans and taught them about compassion as a source of happiness. Dalai Lama was everything, compassionate, kind, humble, vibrant, but not punctual. He was not usually motivated to do challenging things like studying in his student days. Tenzin once said, "It is only when faced with a difficult challenge or deadline would I begin to study." He was known as a slacker, constantly pushing and studying until the deadline. In his teachings about procrastination, he urged students to prepare so that even if they did that day, there would be no regrets.

A famous French writer, Victor Hugo, also found it hard to stay on his task. It is common for writers to procrastinate, and the famous ones were not exempted. Hugo was a chronic procrastinator who would rather do every other thing but focus on his work. Interestingly, he had a unique method of fighting procrastination. Sometimes he asked his servant to strip him naked and never return the clothes until a particular time. That was some drastic action taken to stave off procrastination for good.

Another interesting procrastination story was that of Saint Augustine, who had to stop his sexual desires but kept procrastinating. Although Augustine has Bob Dylan, who penned down his lyrics, he still had a way of falling into distractions. Augustine often fell into sin, forgot the sacred path of being a Christian, and was only pronounced a saint later in life. This was after he found his way out of his sinful life, a task that took him a long time to get done.

Examining these famous people, we can see that first. They had to be aware of their situation and the manner they procrastinate. They accepted that it was a default that had to be removed and understood the habit as a blocker standing in the way of their goals. This created a motivation to take actions that snapped them out of the shackles of procrastination.

These are genuine processes to freedom that I wish to project in the later chapters of this book. You must accept your situation, consider the reasons for your goals, get motivated, and take actions that will help you quit postponing your tasks no matter how challenging they may seem.

Awareness is the first step toward change. Eric Hoffer once said, "*To become different from what we are, we must have some awareness of what we are.*" If you skip this awareness stage, whatever change you must have experienced is merely incidental. We can simply call that a change of mind, and since you haven't figured out the triggers, you will still return to such acts. Being aware of what you are doing wrong in your life? Why you procrastinate, how you do it and when you do it is the kind of awareness we need here. Even if you have stopped procrastinating at the moment, you still need to ask yourself this question;

Did you really quit, or did you just change?

Let's take, for example, a man who loves to gamble. He must understand how much money he had lost to gambling and how it affected his financial security or hindered his goals. The man must make a conscious decision to quit. Before this decision, he must have understood his triggers and found ways to resist them. Then, make sure that he never gives in to these triggers so that he is not going back to gambling again. He must have developed willpower that helps him face the temptation with utmost determination.

If this gambler is unaware of all these, he will just be on autopilot and follow all triggers and impulses that lead him back to gambling again. This time is more likely to fall deeper into the action than before he attempted to stop. If he is aware and has developed the willpower to quit, the thought of the repercussions of gambling will be his best guide to shunning the triggers. The more knowledge he can gather about his gambling habit, the more chances he has to resist the urge.

Like excessive gambling, procrastination is a habit. Changing this behaviour goes beyond mere awareness. You must be aware of the triggers, put them off, and build the willpower to stop for good before you can be free. This willpower is the stage you get motivated. You discover the reasons for your goals and objectives. That is how badly you need to complete that project, stop a habit, or study. It is the benefits you gain from achieving any task ahead of you.

The Art of Self-Awareness

Self-awareness is your most critical stage in this journey to quitting procrastination. According to[1] Shelley Duval and Robert Wicklund, "Self-awareness is the ability to focus on yourself and how your actions, thoughts, or emotions do or align with your internal standards. If you're highly self-aware, you can objectively evaluate yourself, manage your emotions, align your behaviour with your values, and understand how others perceive you correctly." This simply means that if you are self-aware, you will be able to interpret your feelings, actions, and thoughts.

I see it as a means to assess your growth and effectiveness and stay conscious of everything you do. With self-awareness, you will be able to organize yourself better and decide the qualities you wish to let go of, and in the long-term, figure out the best way to become a changed person. It gives you complete control over your decisions and builds more confidence as you fight off procrastination. There are two types of self-awareness.

1. Shelley Duval, Robert A. Wicklund (1972): A Theory Objective Self Awareness

Private Awareness

This is how you see yourself and clearly optimize your values, passions, aspirations, feelings, strengths, and weaknesses and the impact it has on you and others. If you have private self-awareness, you become introspective about your feelings and reactions. When something different happens to you, you can attribute it to certain things that change around you. For instance, you get an opportunity to work on a large project but suddenly start to become tense and sacred. Your ability to attribute this feeling to the new task ahead of you is private self-awareness. You just know that this is how you feel when you get a large project. Feelings like this can be used both negatively and positively. They can become triggers to motivation or procrastination. We shall emphasize this in a future chapter of the book.

Public Awareness

In this case, you are aware of how people see you and often choose to maintain every socially acceptable standard. People with this kind of self-awareness are usually more concerned about what people think about them and often become pleasers. It can also lead to evaluation anxiety, a situation whereby you are distressed or worried about how people perceive you. This may not completely align with procrastination. But, in a case where you are publicly aware of yourself, you will do everything possible to ensure that people don't perceive you to be a time-waster or lazy. Hence, instead of procrastinating meeting times, you just head straight to the meeting room. You will also get on the project or study earlier than the deadline because you don't want to be called a failure.

You need to balance on the beam of self-awareness. Do not fall into the temptation of valuing one over the other. You must see yourself clearly and get feedback from others to better understand.

Becoming self-aware

You can't stop procrastination if you are not self-aware. Trust me; this is not some regular inspirational quote but a genuine piece of truth. Self-awareness explains your successes and failures, so with this, you can easily map out those actions that hinder your ability to get your task done without postponement. These are proven strategies that will help you develop your understanding of yourself.

- **Meditate**

Like most people, you are aware that meditation is a practice that gives you more and more knowledge about yourself at every point in time. Honestly, you don't need to do the traditional inhale and exhale kind of meditation. Just create a little time for a pause or reflection. You can do this immediately you wake up in the morning or before you fall asleep at night. It depends on what time you know you concentrate better. Ask yourself questions like, "*What am I trying to achieve? What is holding me back? What is slowing me down? What can I do to change?*" If you can have this figured out, you will begin to light up the dark spots in your life and have a clearer view of your procrastination status.

- **Note your key plans and priorities.**

You can't go wrong with writing down what you plan to do and arranging them in order of priority. This will help you figure out quickly when deviating from significant tasks. Keep track of both the large tasks and the minor ones. It would seem tempting to ignore little things like sending an official email or reminders, but omitting them due to constant procrastination may have a negative effect in the end.

- **Get Feedback from friends and relations.**

This reflects public awareness. You cannot tell how you come across to others unless they give you feedback. Let your friends play the honest mirror and give you a critical and objective perspective about the type of person you are. You can approach them by saying, "Hey, I need you to give me an honest response. How bad is my procrastination. Please be straight with me?" or you come up straight with, "I know I procrastinate a lot. Can you tell me each time I do that so I can learn to stop?"

However, these strategies must be applied in the different stages of self-awareness and help you achieve your end goal, which is figuring out your motivation and actions that will reduce procrastination. These are the three levels of self-awareness.

Identify your thoughts and emotions.

Observing this level will help determine if emotions are the roots of your procrastination. Hence, regulating your emotions will help you stop procrastinating. Whenever you find yourself postponing a task, you will be able to ask yourself if it is the right kind of delay or caused by fear. Recognizing your emotions will help you address them with reactions that spell them out. We often feel negative emotions lessen[2] once we have them spelt out. While you meditate, get a paper and write down your emotions at that moment. If you search through and can't figure out words to describe your emotions, you can write down any thought that sounds like a judgement and then make it a question. Try to revise the emotions every hour to see if you still feel them. Try to take this exercise in a quiet place so that your emotions don't get influenced by new stimuli initiated by music or any other noise around you.

Know your beliefs

2. Stuart Wolpert (2007): Putting Feelings Into Words Produces Therapeutic Effects in the Brain

Most times, your brain thinks of the future as something not relatively essential, so procrastinating brings you relief but more pressure and stress in the future. Procrastinators see the next hour, day or week as a long time that doesn't need to be planned at the moment. So even when you push a task to the next day, you will still hesitate to plan and stay determined to complete the job. There is a need to close this gap between the present and future. To achieve this, you must record your beliefs. Taking a note to journal this in five minutes is the best way to start.

One approach is to write down the answer to the question you wrote when identifying your thoughts and provide solutions to these questions. For example, if you have written down, "Is this project difficult? Then, write the answers honestly and express what you think about the project. Another approach is to spell out the event that triggers your emotions, your belief about the event, and the consequences, which means the belief makes you feel. For example, when you get an unexpected task (event), you may think you believe your boss gave you the task because you always appear idle (belief), and then you feel you are a pushover (consequences).

With this, you can choose to change your belief about events so that you can arrive at a different feeling towards them. Then, your motivation to complete tasks will begin to grow stronger than previous feelings that cause you to postpone it.

Track your emotions

Understand that you will pay the price in the future for the time wasted now. It often comes with the feeling of shame, and then you try to bury the mistake but continue to procrastinate more. The best way to get out of this is to break the cycle, take a clean slate and start over. Pardon your bad decisions, and forgive yourself for procrastinating. The only way to get this done is to keep a record of them and become aware of them. Create an accountability chart. This is where you write three important tasks for the day as you start your day and a time slot for all you did that day at the end of the day. With this, you can track what you have done and what you haven't.

Then, look critically at those things you didn't accomplish and begin the process again, taking note of each level.

Every strategy or idea for self-awareness mentioned in this chapter is useless without practice. After reading through it, do not procrastinate your start date or time. Get started now and let it gradually become a daily task so that you build a solid awareness of yourself and the status of procrastinating. Pay attention to your thoughts, beliefs and decisions each day and see how closer to giving up procrastination for good. With awareness well-structured, motivation becomes easier by the day. If for any reason you wake up feeling lazy about meditating and getting your thought, beliefs and decisions tracked, you must know that it's procrastination that still has a grip on you and not laziness.

Procrastination is not Laziness.

Here is one misconception that many have, and it keeps them confused about what to fight against. People assume procrastination is laziness or that it is caused by laziness. If you think this way, you will find it difficult to eradicate procrastination for good. Hence, we need to clarify these two so that you will be sure of what you are fighting against in future chapters.

Procrastination is the act of always postponing decisions and actions. It simply means creating a delay on specific tasks and goals to do them right before the deadline without any concrete reason.

This delay can be associated with academic performance, finance, emotions, or mental health. It usually ends with an outcome that has a negative effect on your goal or achievement. These delays are intentional even when you are willing to do things on time. But laziness is your unwillingness to put effort at all into a task. This is someone who never writes his monthly reports at work or a student who never does his assignment. It is possible to procrastinate even when you are not lazy.

You just keep doing other things that give your pleasure and ignore the main task that you have concluded to be difficult. Or you purposely delay the task because you can't figure out where to start. But a lazy person might start without delay but still never finish because they refuse to put in the effort. While a procrastinator still completes the task with the pressure of meeting a deadline, a lazy person ignores the task. Procrastination is not a choice, your task ignites negative emotions, and you get a natural instinct to ignore it. But, for laziness, you just don't feel like doing the task at all. As a procrastinator, you have a goal and high standard ambitions that you want to achieve but still have a lot of distractions to fight with.

So, if you feel held back from activities, you need to figure out what is holding you back. If you feel tired, stressed out with emotions, or physically restricted, you will most likely procrastinate to a period you think is the best time to complete the task. But if you just don't feel interested in the whole activity and would rather do without, you are fighting with laziness.

In the next chapter, let's dive deeper into our understanding of procrastination.

Chapter 2
AWARENESS

In the previous chapter, we have been fishing out the techniques for awareness and its relation to motivation and actions. Here, I will further guide you through the awareness stage. As I said, it is the first step to any form of change. To be fully aware, you must be sure that a light bulb lights your mind. You must know how much procrastinating has cost you and what it may cost you in the future. Then you can see the ladder before you, your current position, and the necessary steps to climb higher or lower. When you are aware of your situation, you will be able to stop self-deceit, take full responsibility for yourself, and start your revolution. For this to happen, I will provide all the information you need about the causes of procrastination, its negative consequences, and the differences between good and bad procrastination.

In all honours, let's tell ourselves the truth. Truth and awareness are brothers from a mother who always complement each other. If you are not open to the truth, you will never reach that level of awareness that will bring you genuine change. Without the truth, there is no essence in fighting procrastination because, in due time, you will get tired, and there will be no zeal to change. I have to reveal to you nine hidden truths about procrastination. The more you know about your problem, the easier it is to fight them. Knowledge is a weapon that can be used to build and also destroy.

Things You Need To Know About Procrastination

There are good things and bad things. So which one will you like to hear first? Come on, don't let the temptation to push this until tomorrow overcome. I know I am here until tomorrow, but you need this knowledge every day before tomorrow. I will begin with the bad news and let the sweet ones come later so they can last longer in your mind.

Procrastination is always known before failure. It is the centre of most unfinished tasks and failed projects. Suppose you are not getting the desired results in anything you have done. In that case, there is a probability that you have continuously postponed specific engagements that needed to be carried out at one point or the other. Hence, you delayed the steps to the project's success and now have to rush through them as the deadline approaches. This is the bad news. Then, the good news is that a procrastinator is usually mentally sophisticated. They are genius rebels who constantly create obstacles for their own goal. Don't feel offended! That is the truth I need you to know. As a procrastinator, you are continually creating setbacks and shooting your own feet at the slightest opportunity.

These things I need you to know about procrastination are both good and bad things that would guide you and assist your decision to get rid of the habit for good.

1. Procrastinating always seems cool.

Imagine this! You pay your bills before the deadline. You prepare for your exams one week ahead, complete projects weeks before the deadline, grocery shop before the shelves become empty, and buy Christmas gifts in October. How boring! There is no fun in the stress of planning and following all plans to the letter. We are genius rebels. We need to feel that urgent discharge of adrenaline with an impending deadline and closing dates. You think there is a need to enjoy the uncertainty of the last moment. If these are your thought about putting off until tomorrow, they are lies you must unlearn.

Some people think that procrastination improves creativity. Because even if they have projects and get stuck with pushing the start and finish date forward, they still do a great job. One thing they miss out on is that they could have done better if the job wasn't rushed. There will be moments when the adrenaline rush will not lead to a perfect round-up, and the job will be left incomplete or cancelled. Some even consider that situation another benefit as it helps them conserve resources. There is also a belief that procrastinating gives them time to think, helps them work more efficiently, increases their feelings of control, and increases motivation.

The truth is that these benefits are not guaranteed[3] in any way. For example, a student who procrastinates on a project or exam can enjoy reduced stress initially but experience more pressure as the deadline approaches. Hence the benefit here is only for a while. Some think it will give them a feeling of control, whereas they experience the opposite. Procrastination is more expensive than you mostly believe it can be and should not be mistaken to be something cool even as you enjoy it.

2. Procrastination is serious

It is a real thing! Even while you do it, you know deep within you that postponing continuously could create problems in the future. At some point, you begin to make excuses when anyone asks for feedback or even try to cover up with a lie. Everything is an excuse for a procrastinator to skip a task until another day, knowing fully

3. Dianne M Tice, Roy F. Baumeister (1997): Longitudinal Study of Procrastination, Performance, Stress, and Health: The Costs and Benefits of Dawdling

well that they could have created an alternative against the blocker used as an excuse. Often, procrastinators do not make that habit serious enough even to see it as a tragedy.

Some mistake procrastination for purposeful delay[4] as well. A purposeful delay comes with strategic and rational reasons why a task cannot be carried out at that time. It also could be in a situation where the deadline for the project is still far off, and delaying will not cause any adverse outcomes. But procrastination comes with excuses that are majorly manufactured to avoid feeling guilty about falling under distractions.

In our society today, pleasure is always a priority over duty. Meanwhile, procrastination is a relevant social and personal problem that should never be overlooked. It pervades every scope of one's life and pushes us towards pushing aside responsibilities. When it starts manifesting in the life of teenagers and adolescents, as it often does, it should be suppressed and taken seriously because it often becomes a bigger problem as the individual matures.

3. Procrastination is not a problem of time management

Procrastination should not be mistaken for time management. Some people who see that they procrastinate begin to consume all sorts of professional and self-development articles that promise to help them through their time management problems. That is another complete waste of time. *Trust me; I speak from experience!*

Procrastination means knowing what you are supposed to do to reach your goal, but you still don't do it. Sometimes procrastination results from time management, and other times it is caused by poor self-care. Procrastination is an emotional problem. It doesn't mean

4. Haghbin Mohsen (2015): Conceptualization and Operationalization of Delay: Development and Validation of the Multifaceted Measure of Academic Procrastination and the Delay Questionnaire

you are doing a task and taking too long to complete it. It means you are seated and ready to commence, but the thought of the complex procedure creeps into your mind, and you decide to skip the tasks until tomorrow. Most time, unnecessary things like painting your nails, checking phone notifications, or watching social media take control of your time, and you end up with excuses like, "*I don't have the inspiration I need.*", "*This project is too difficult.*", "*I need some air, and I will work on this tomorrow.*" More excuses come up until you are comfortable with picking another date to do your tasks. Interestingly, the cycle goes on until you are close to the deadline and or you can't complete the task anymore.

In the case of time management, you make a list of what you need to do. You get it done at a more extended duration compared to what you need. Someone with time management problems will be seeking ways to increase their work speed to complete more tasks, unlike a procrastinator who will be seeking to stop postponing delegated duties and responsibilities.

4. You are not born a procrastinator; you become one.

Let's get rid of phrases like, "*But that's how I am," I've been like this since I was little." It's my character," "I cannot change," or "I will still do it even if I postpone to tomorrow.*" You should make yourself a feast of this kind of life. But if that is what you choose, I will advise you to stop reading at this point. This book is for people who have seen that procrastination is a problem hindering their ability to achieve certain goals.

Procrastination is never inborn. It is a habit you have developed over time, and until it begins to hinder so many goals you should achieve, you may never see it as a problem. It starts from postponing little things like laundry, cleaning, grocery shopping, and others to postponing projects—studying for meetings, preparation for presentations, or interviews. Procrastination is not a personality trait that you inherit from genes. Joseph Ferrari[5] made it clear that procrastination is learned and not inborn. It is something you learnt to do to avoid the responsibility of completing or starting a task.

Although procrastination can be a byproduct of your upbringing or environment, it is something you nurture and can be changed. It is time for you to unlearn the bad habit and take control of your personality. Do not let this bad habit that you nurture define your identity.

5. Procrastinators are serial liars.

Procrastinators generally tend to lie to others and themselves. They conveniently console themselves with fabricated facts just to get away from performing their task at that minute. One common lie is, " *I don't feel like doing it today. Tomorrow is better.*" The truth is that they say the same thing every day until the deadline. Another is, "*It is better to do this at the last minute as I work better under pressure.*" Some procrastinators feel that waiting until the last minute will spike up their creativity and ability to think so that they can complete the task efficiently. Come On! You are just seeking a valid excuse to skip the task. The truth for that lie is that waiting till the last minute will create invisible costs. Another common lie is, "*Delay for a day of weeks will not change anything.*" Every delay comes with a price in the long run. That one day you choose to delay may not have a significant effect, but in the long run, the number of days you delay will snowball into a huge impact.

You need to be exposed to the devastating effects of procrastination, and if you don't postpone this chapter any further, you will get to read about the impact soon.

5. Joseph R. Ferrari, Vincent DePaul Distinguished Professor of Psychology: " Procrastination and Task Avoidance - Theory, Research and Treatment "

6. Procrastinators are artists of distractions.

Procrastinators are incredibly proactive with things that distract them. These distractions do not require any mental or physical effort. They are mostly things they enjoy doing for pleasure, like checking their mail, verifying every notification on their Facebook page, spend time watching specific television programs or video games. These are junks that take up the time of procrastinators and make them too busy to do their tasks that day until tomorrow.

These distractions affect procrastinators just as methadone on junkies. It lowers the anxiety related to the fear of losing their job, getting broke, or failing. They enjoy the moment with great pleasure and pay dearly for it later.

7. Procrastinators think of it like a mountain.

Honestly, procrastinators overthink every situation and devise excuses that will help them skip the task. They think about how to organize their task, how to complete them, deadlines, possible consequences, and possible challenges. And the more they believe, the more the task seems to be too big to begin at the moment. Then, they start postponing. If you are an overthinker, you need to start from the unbecoming one before you embark on this journey to quit procrastination. Overthinking turns your proactive thoughts into worries and large mountains of blockers you need to pull down.

Get lost in your work and not your thoughts. Learn to start with the little tasks first, no matter how large the project is. Instead of dwelling on the possibility of you being unable to meet the deadline, break the objectives into smaller pieces and take up the most straightforward task on the list daily. Then, you will be able to sort it all out.

8. Procrastinators are not always perfectionists.

For several reasons, perfectionists are always looking for an excuse to pend their tasks. They seek the perfect exam, the perfect article, the perfect project, and most times, the perfect time to start work. These are equally some of the perfect excuses of procrastinators, which often make a mistake themselves for perfectionists. You need to unbelieve that because if you keep postponing until the deadline, you will end up with an incomplete project or an unperfect job.

An analysis was conducted on 71 students by Prof. Steel 5 to compare procrastination in education. The research established that true perfectionists are not procrastinators.

9. Procrastination correlates with a study.

A study conducted on university students shows that 90% of them suffer from procrastination, and 75% are usually affected by procrastination. I can confirm that most of them also read articles about rapid learning techniques; meanwhile, procrastination is their primary problem.

If you are a student currently, I believe you have skipped studying so many times that you have forwarded your studies for different reasons. Although, sometimes, more genuine excuses spring up as health challenges. College students who frequently have colds, gastrointestinal problems, insomnia, influenza, and others tend to procrastinate. Procrastinating as a student can frustrate teamwork and create resentment among friends and colleagues.

Now that you have clarity on this dark beast called procrastination, you must understand the possible reasons why you are always postponing your tasks.

Because we procrastinate

Most times, you have thought about you the possibility of doing a task the next day, but as that time draws nearer, you find yourself looking for an avenue to skip the task. Every time these happen, try to reflect on that day's activities and pick out the moment you decided to postpone the task. For example; "*Tomorrow, I have to deliver a project, and within five days I have an exam, yet I checked my email 227 times, planted 4 hectares of dwarf beets on Farmville game, and found out that all my friends have made friends with Sare1 That's all I did.*" With this example, the procrastinator will eventually shift for several reasons and doesn't realize that he has distracted himself with games, email notifications, and gist with friends. I can go on and on with different psychologies and theories that explain why you procrastinate, but I will limit the reasons to these four.

You enjoy the pleasure that comes with excitement.

Checking your phone notifications from Facebook or email gives you instant gratification. A new message can show you new likes that will ignite your self-esteem and novelty, giving you instant pleasure and satisfaction. You feel so good at that moment that you get lost in wandering around social media for more excitement. So many American nerds understood the feelings, and they provided enough flow of excitement for people to enjoy, which in the long run built them a billionaire's empire.

There is nothing terrible in satisfying these minor weaknesses, as long as they don't jeopardize your future happiness. That joy comes with you passing your exams, completing a project, or starting a new line of business. But the truth is, most times, continuously surrendering to these excitements means that you will keep postponing your commitments, projects, dreams, and others. You also tell yourself it is not that serious, that you have time, and that tomorrow you will continue. However, the process repeats itself again tomorrow.

Fear

Sometimes we postpone our tasks because of fear. It could be fear of failure or success, new responsibility, changes, uncertainty and many others. They are so many as they can fill up an entire book. The point is that fear and procrastination are two different focuses, but they work together. The more fears you are, the more likely you are to procrastinate and the more you procrastinate, the more your fear. So if you keep postponing that big project you are scared of because you doubt your capability, you will end up being scared of not meeting up with the deadline. Procrastination helps to increase your fear until it is denser and denser. So every time you postpone your task, you feel relief, but the truth is, you have only moved reality forward as the fear still comes the next time. Then, as usual, the circle goes on and on.

Unclear Ideas

Another reason you procrastinate is that our ideas for the task seem vague. Since the target is not clear enough, you continue postponing it to tomorrow. In this case, you have a project you must complete but do not know where to begin. This blocker seems to be like an invisible wall between you and success. At this block, you start to divert into other distractions like playing the Farmville game or checking posts on Facebook, videos on Instagram and others. The solution to this is quite straightforward, just get a paper and outline the task in small bits to help you achieve your goal. But those who procrastinate for this reason are more likely to plan every micro-activity, waste hours on creating a perfect plan and end up not doing any.

Overoptimistic

When it comes to completing a task, procrastinators often overestimate their capacity. They believe that tomorrow, they will magically perform their task and turn into good students and productive employees that can complete the job they have been postponing for days in the blink of an eye. If you think this way, you are just trying to suppress the feeling of guilt that has enveloped you. Then, you place yourself under the illusion that you can postpone the task and still do it later without facing the consequences of procrastination. Some studies6 have established that if we tend to underestimate the duration of future activities to be short, then we are bad planners. If you are too optimistic about your ability, you tend to procrastinate with the belief that you can do much to complete the task in a short time before the deadline.

Before we go into the cost of procrastination, I would like to consolidate your awareness by explaining the concept tied to your postponement and the future, which is our worst enemy.

Procrastination, Return to the Future, and the bales space

The movie "Back to the Future" is undoubtedly one of my favourite Hollywood movies, and it always helps me remember the significant melancholy of my childhood. Recently, I looked back at another movie, "Trilogy," and thought about the key concept of understanding how to defeat procrastination, which I would like to report in this guide.

The Ego Future

In the episode of Trilogy, the hero, Marty McFly (the unforgettable Michael J. Fox), is catapulted from the calm and comforting 1985 to 2015 that involved hoverboards and flying cars. Just imagine if you get the chance to go 30 years in the future. Naturally, you will picture yourself as a successful businessman, rockstar, or professor. For Marty, he was hit by a nasty surprise. Before seeing the future, he fantasized about being a successful man that Sara would love, but he bitterly discovered that he had turned into a perfect man failed of half age.

Many of us are convinced that the future[6] will be highly motivated, concentrated and productive. Also, we have ambitious plans but invariably discover that reality is always a little worse than how much we expect. Then, we start depending on the future.

One ugly news is that your future is unmotivated, distracted and lazy right from the moment you put off your responsibility and load it on the shoulders of your future. You should take your life into your hands at this moment and deprive procrastination of all its powers on you.

The Cost of Procrastination

In this section, we will see how bad procrastination is and how it can benefit you. If you are still reading this guide, it is simply because procrastination has cost you something at one point. A voice in your head keeps telling you that you are wasting your life and that you could do much more. This uncomfortable feeling and thought

6. Michael M. Roy And Nicholas J. S. Christenfeld: "*Bias in memory predicts bias in estimation of future task duration*".

are not enough to push you to act. But, when the moment of reality arrives and you experience the consequences of procrastination, you become aware of its real cost, even for those that have never experienced it yet. I have made it my duty to open your mind to the cost of postponing your task to tomorrow.

- **Procrastination defines your self-esteem.**

Every time you postpone your study, work or commitments, you are simply telling yourself that you can't complete such an ambiguous task. You are saying that you do not have the mental, physical or emotional capacity to push through. Hence the best thing is to keep postponing until you seem fit. Procrastination also communicates that an individual is lazy, unmotivated and inconclusive of their true self. It puts your self-esteem on trial as you continue to put off your task. It makes you forget your actual capacity and abilities. You begin to let your strength be defined by thoughts like, "This project is too difficult., " I can't do this yet. I need more time.". These thoughts are excuses you have laid done to procrastinate your task. The gradual start to seem like the true you.

- **Procrastination steals your life.**

As I mentioned in the last paragraph, procrastination steals the real you. Postponing something is scary as it makes the task more important than it should have been in reality. Pushing it forward for too long makes the task require more time, resources, and energy to complete. This is because you could have spread the task into smaller bits to make them simpler. But since you were procrastinating, you have to do everything at once. You lose your free time, hobbies, and passions to that single project.

- **Procrastination takes away serenity.**

Sometimes, you postpone with the illusion of not thinking about the task for a bit until the deadline. But it always happens on the contrary. Whenever you postpone something you have to do, you think about it as a debt you owe. You have only procrastinated to increase your stress and pressure to do the work. So, as the deadline draws near, you have to complete the work in a hurry and then blame the turnout on the stress and pressure. Deep within you, you would have done a better job if you had started earlier in a relaxed state.

- **Procrastination deprives you of your dreams.**

You have targets, ambitions and goals, so when you choose to postpone your tasks continuously for fear or other reasons, you do so for your dreams too. You sabotage yourself deliberately every time you postpone or put off your task. Unknowingly, you create the failure you are scared of in the future. Now you should feel an unfathomable sensation of unease, knowing fully well the repercussions of your constant's procrastinations. It is a boulder tied up on your ankle and causes you to sink, depriving you of pursuing your dreams.

Nevertheless, procrastination has its benefits, and there are times when procrastinating can help you improve certain things.

Benefits of procrastination

Warning: This section will offer a foothold for those that are convinced that procrastination is the right thing. I'm sure you are not one of those, and you will interpret this section correctly without using it as an excuse to keep postponing.

Our life follows a specific rhythm which is the rhythm of the breath. There are moments when we breathe in (productive moments) and when we need to exhale (moments of rest). To insist that every moment of our existence must be productive means we are against nature. The ancient Romans knew the importance of distinguishing *negotium* – the whole time for business activities from the *otium* – which is the rest period.

Idleness and voluntary procrastination of work activities are sometimes necessary to obtain the proper equilibrium in life. But, when resting and idleness begin to be dominant in all your days, you have a problem of laziness. An imbalance is created, and unfunctional leisure moments make black holes that take away your energy and motivation.

To get the greatest benefits from rest and idleness, it must follow productivity and not precede it. Also, to get the best result, you must work with complete focus and the spirit of productivity at 100% before the thing of taking a break.

TEST: The Procrastinators

Scholars and psychologists have identified dozens and different types of procrastinators: the dreamer, the perfectionist, the artist of the leak, the rebel, the warrior, the adventurer, the distressed, the undecided, the scared, the teenager, and the impulsive. If you check the internet, you will find many articles with more definitions for procrastinators. For this guide, we will focus on the simple classifications used by Prof. Solomon and Rothblum in one of their study conducted in 1984[7]. The identified two main groups of procrastinators;

- Relaxed Procrastinators
- Worried Procrastinators

7. Laura J. Solomon And Esther D. Rothblum (1984): "*Academic Procrastination: Frequency and Cognitive- Behavioral Correlates*".

But before we go into the description of these two types, you must complete this test. Kindly follow the instruction below.

Instructions:

There are 10 affirmations. Simply choose 5 that best describe you (not 4 or 6). Do not overthink whether you are right or wrong. Identify your procrastinator profile, as it will help you understand which technique will work for you to stop procrastinating.

Complete the test and sum up the numbers from the affirmations. Let's say you have chosen numbers 2, 4, 6, 7, and 10, then sum it up as 2+4+6+7+10 = 29. This is not a scientific value but just to help you focus on your reality. Let's begin.

1. Life is often too complicated.
2. Before you ask for a date from the girl of your dream, you must have a gun to your head.
3. You often regret childhood when all seemed straightforward.
4. You do not like to be the centre of attention or pick up your responsibility.
5. You are willing to commit yourself to success
6. You often wonder about your scope of life.
7. Facebook is your second home, and it distracts you easily.
8. You have many passions but have never taken any seriously.
9. You have good resolutions at the beginning of every year, but they vanish before the 15th of January.
10. You work better under pressure and close to deadlines.

Score: _______________

Relaxed Procrastinator

This is someone who avoids every cost of boring activities or forces them out of their comfort. They put pleasure ahead and are always able to find an infinite distraction even while doing a task. A classic example of a procrastinator is an off-site student who prefers to chill out by going to parties with friends instead of preparing for exams coming up the following day. Another trait of a relaxed procrastinator is someone impatient for results and who wants to see everything immediately after a project starts.

Worried Procrastinator

A worried procrastinator is a person that avoids anything that puts them in s stressful situation. He prefers a simple street to wind tents on a mountain pebble. An example is a student that has postponed the exam preparations until the last day and yet wanders the room as prey to anxiety, taking a frequent bath and breaks to relax. The fear of failure and success is common in this type of procrastinator. They often pose unrealistic goals and exhibit some perfectionism.

Yeah! Now I have to reveal the result of your test. I am sure you have already figured this out from the description above. Well, if you score less than 25, there is a good chance that you have the features of a worried procrastinator. On the other hand, if you score above 25, there are chances that you are a relaxed procrastinator. Where do you find yourself?

Chapter 3
Motivation

Here you are! I'm glad you didn't put off this chapter to tomorrow. That means you are determined and ready to change this habit. Hence, I'm excited to be pushing through this success barrier with you.

For this chapter, you must turn up that lamp of awareness. Yes, there is a lamp in you that needs a spark. Imagine you have a set of newspaper sheets that you need to burn. Even if you add enough fuel and dry wood, you can't get the flame up until you get a spark. The spark from a lighter or matches will give you your first flame.

Now you are aware of the cost of procrastination, its benefits and the possible reasons why you are procrastinating. You know there is something wrong with your kind of choices and attitudes to complex tasks. That is the spark you need to get motivated. Kudos! There are many others out there and even some of your friends who are not aware that they are procrastinators. Some are also experts, giving endless excuses and explanations as to why they skipped their tasks. Even worse, some friends who may have told you squarely that you procrastinate are also guilty but unaware.

Research carried out on a certain level of students proved that 80%-95% of college students procrastinate, but only 50% considered procrastination a problem. Judging by these numbers, we can say that many out there know the meaning of procrastination and are not aware that they are also procrastinators. I will relate this first stage of knowing you have a problem to the stage of gathering the newspaper sheet to burn. You still need a spark to make it burn out[8].

Getting a spark to burn your mess is where motivation comes in. The spark swings you into action and helps you defeat procrastination. Let's relate this again to burning newspaper sheets. You have gathered the shit in the stage of awareness. Then you look for a lighter to start a fire which is your motivation. Before motivation is correct, your awareness stage must be complete to the point that you are also aware of what can give you that spark. When you get the spark, the action begins as the newspaper sheets start to burn.

We need to find your lost motivation, and in this chapter, I will propose a simple and practical technique to help you find motivation daily. With this daily motivation, burning out the procrastination habit will become easier. The methods are associated with the different types of procrastination that we have. So, you must understand the two kinds of procrastination.

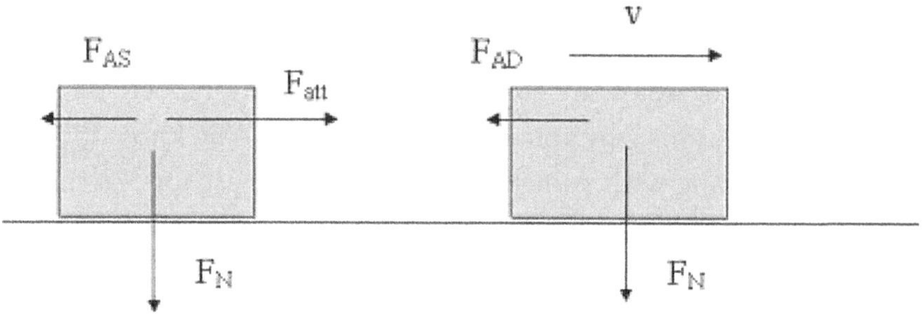

8. Qun G. Jiao1, Denise A. DaRos-Voseles2, Kathleen M. T. Collins3, et al: "Academic procrastination and the performance of graduate-level cooperative groups in research methods courses"

The Physics of "postponement": Static and Dynamic Procrastination

I know the question popping in your head now is, why physics? Yea, I command we go to physics because that was my favourite. I look like a nerd now, but seriously, the laws regulating the universe have a charm on everything. They can be applied to our social life and also used to explain some scope of psychology.

One example is the frictional force when you try to glide or roll one solid object over another. It occurs when you try to push your sofa to another corner of the living room without lifting it or when you have a moving motorcycle. There are two types of frictional friction that are closely related to procrastination. They are Static and Dynamic friction. So, where you have to push a sofa is the static friction and the motorcycle moving over an object is the dynamic friction.

Like the frictional force, procrastination is a force that opposes our movement toward our main target. It pulls you to slow you down and restricts you from meeting your goals. Sometimes this force extends as far as limiting the goals you set for yourself. Also, like frictional force, we experience procrastination differently depending on the different kinds of tasks that we have to do. Hence, this brings us to the two types of procrastination: static and dynamic.

Static Procrastination

Anything static is likely to be a massive blockage for other things. It means it is solid enough to restrict any movement unless there is enough pressure. This can be related to that feeling of stiffness you experience anytime you want to start a new business, resume a new workplace or start a new school. You have all your ideas laid out in a sheet before you, but you still keep forwarding the following action.

Static procrastination can happen to anyone. It is that type of procrastination where you know what to do but can't get yourself to begin the task. Instead, you keep pushing it to tomorrow. It is dangerous because it makes it difficult for you to meet your goals. Let's take, for example, a man that wants to start a shoe business. He had his plans laid out, and all she had to do was begin with registering the company on the online marketplace, ordering the goods to market and implementing strategies to sell the shoes. Every day he sets his mind to write his business name, and at the end of each day, he keeps putting it off until tomorrow for one reason or another.

He may never get to start this new business in three months, six months, or even a year because he remains static and unable to push himself to take a step.

Dynamic Procrastination

This type of procrastination comes from distractions that slow you down as you work on your projects, tasks, study, and other difficult activities. Although the dynamic distractions are not massive blocks like static, it doesn't mean they are less dangerous. It comes with distractions that can make your project take longer or impossible to complete. Little distractions like checking a quick message on your phone can lead to watching videos on social media until you get lost in the moment and put off your task till tomorrow. The more space we give distractions as we carry out tasks, the more likely it is for us to get bogged down!

Having understood the differences between static and dynamic procrastination, you'll agree that we need different techniques for the two types of procrastination and the types of motivation required to eradicate them. Don't get tired or distracted. I've got your attention glued up to this point, and it will sadden me to see that you procrastinate the next phase of the chapter till tomorrow.

Yeah! Let's continue since you are still here.

So many books, poems, and quotes have been written to help people find their motivations. I believe this is not the first time you will be reading about it. But I wish you see this differently and take every piece of advice in this book because the secret of motivation is hidden in your beautiful view. You probably think, "*I hope you aren't trying to fool me.*" You have read so many motivating books, but the secret to finding motivation that will defeat your habit of always postponing is under your eyes. Get paper and a pen. Spell out "Motivation." It is a word that you wrote down so many times. But if you look closely, you will find this:

MotivAction

Motivation is generally known to be the desire that drives individuals towards pursuing a goal or achievement. But here, I put it to you that motivation simply means *Reasons and Action.* Without a motive, there can't be a desire to drive action. Before you took the action of reading this book, you already had a reason which was to stop procrastinating. Knowing the meaning of your actions is not enough for you to get motivated to do them. You have to be pushed by the reason for taking such action. That's what makes a full motivation. Let's break it down further.

Reasons

Many dictionaries define reason as a cause or basis for doing something, and I agree. It is the drive you need to act and achieve your goals. It is also what you need to neutralize static and dynamic procrastination for good. Reasons arise from asking Why? Why would I want to start a keto diet? Why do I need to stay up late to complete your project? Why do you need to read a chapter every night? Think of all the whys connected to that action you have been procrastinating. Make sure you find a reason for that action. If you can't find a reason for your actions, then you will not be able to stop procrastinating. That reason is a founding pillar to building your motivation.

Maybe you enrolled in that gym to reduce fat and shed some weight. Your reason could be that you want to stay healthy and eliminate dangerous body fats. Or that you want to start a career in modelling. Then, you have something that can push you to act.

Have you been finding it challenging to learn even after enrolling in the course for the skill you admire? Then, think of why you want to know. Is it to grow your income or build a career?

Why have you decided to start that new project? Is it to get a promotion? Then, let that cause drive you towards defeating procrastination and taking the first step towards achieving your goal.

The basis for your goal is the *founding pillar* on which you must build your motivation day after day.

Action

As the reasons set your mind to how important that task is, you also need to take action to make the reasons substantial. Your motivation is incomplete if you have not taken steps to achieve your goal. As a procrastinator, you will still experience blockers as you begin the second stage of motivation. But if you have been able to add concrete meaning to why you need the task done, you are less likely to procrastinate taking action. Instead, you will set yourself in motion. Reflect back on the reasons, understand the meaning and find your motivation.

Make it a daily habit to find your reasons and set your actions. For static procrastination, you will break the blocker with motives and actions once and for all. But for dynamic procrastination, you must place the exercise as routine. You should take a dose of motivation daily or even hourly. Remember, dynamic procrastination is on tasks that have started but moving slowly. Constantly motivating yourself will help you speed up to complete the task.

Then, set the motion without making external conditions as excuses. You mustn't wait for some magical electrocution or divine inspiration. If you do, you are setting up another procrastination thread that will keep you stagnant for more years. Such interventions never come. *Simply begin*. Motivation is like a snowflake falling on the side of a mountain. First, it is fragile and small until it rolls down the slope slowly, then faster until it enlarges and becomes an avalanche.

Take live circumstances as they come and live with them. This way, you can decide on your dreams and overcome challenges. Here's a poem titled "*Despite*."

Despite the bitter taste of failures

Despite the fury of bad luck

Despite the unacceptable certainties of your environment

Despite the abyss of demotivation

Despite the burden of fatigue

Despite the unpleasantness of your task

Despite the deceptions of doubt

Despite the advance in years

Despite the smoke of fear

No goal is too ambitious.

Avoiding The Result Trap

Oh wow! With these lines, I believe I have a future as a poet (just kidding, no distractions). Actions can also be a motivation. Things you have experienced in the course of life could trap you in procrastination and demotivate you. And the setbacks you will face in the future can also stand as a blocker to achieving your objectives.

Nevertheless, you must not allow yourself to sink into these blockers. The best way to stay motivated amidst challenges is to understand that growth is not linear. Do not expect you to keep going from one point to another without bumps. It is not enough to commit daily to constant progress.

Linear growth doesn't exist. Just like an electron, you face different periodic challenges when you begin the change process. That means you will meet a period of stalemate when you decide to change your diet, start a new program, create your business or begin a project. At this time, all your efforts may prove abortive, and it seems like you are not progressing. It is a stage of *accumulation* where change is in an embryonic state and grows daily. You must not lose motivation.

The accumulation stage varies depending on the goal you are pursuing. In some cases, you begin to see progress after a few hours, but in other cases, you need years of consistency before you can point out progress. Do not let your motivation get trapped in the drastic result. Minimalize your expectation in progress. Let every tiny improvement feed your inspiration.

How do you measure your progress?

One good way to keep progress on track is to create a *chain*. Mark out your progress in a calendar with an "X" every day you engage with activities that help you reach your objective. Then, create a chain of all the "XS" without missing any. This will help communicate to your subconscious that you are progressing despite the absence of tangible results. At this accumulation stage, this visualization is needed to trigger a circle of Actions – Result – Motivation.

Another is to measure your *climb*. With this, you will be able to measure your progress in achieving your goal. It could be on a white sheet where you draw a triangle with the peak representing your goal. Let the field base represent your condition today. The triangle should show details of how you climb the mountain to the summit, which is your goal. Report each day of progress with the date. Even if you have had a hard day where you fell backwards, indicate it. This climbing triangle will help you understand the level you are at achieving your goal. You will figure out those actions that slow you down and fake steps that don't push you further.

With these two styles of measuring your progress, you can avoid the resulting trap and develop daily motivation. There is yet another technique very effective for defeating procrastination for good.

Finding Motivation through creative visualization

Creative visualization is an imagination tool you don't want to ignore. It is a unique way of using your imagination to create a vivid image of what you want. You can create an image of your future and subject your emotions to these images you have created. "The term Creative visualization" was mentioned by Wallace Wattles in his best seller. "*The science of getting rich,*" which was written in the 20th century. It was also mentioned in a self-help book by Rhone Byrne, "*The Secret.*"

People use these techniques differently, and psychologists have created different stages of creative visualization that work. In the late 1970s, Shaki Gawain wrote about how to use creative visualization. He devised a formula with four stages. The first stage is to choose a goal and then form a mental image of the outcome of what you want. Next, picture this image often throughout the day, add positivity to what you have visualized, and imagine that it is happening at the moment.

You are probably wondering, *Hey Andre, how does this long talk relate to my procrastination and visualization?*

Remember the common saying in Aladdin and the Genius of the lamp, "*Every of your wish for me is an order, Master.*" Remove the lamp and the flying carpet and think of those words as an idea in a creative view. What would you rather be? Let your imagination work like an order.

Numerous scientific experiments have tested the indisputable effectiveness of creative visualization. Here is an example of where some Russian scientists compared four groups of Olympic athletes subjected to different regimes of training which is shown below:

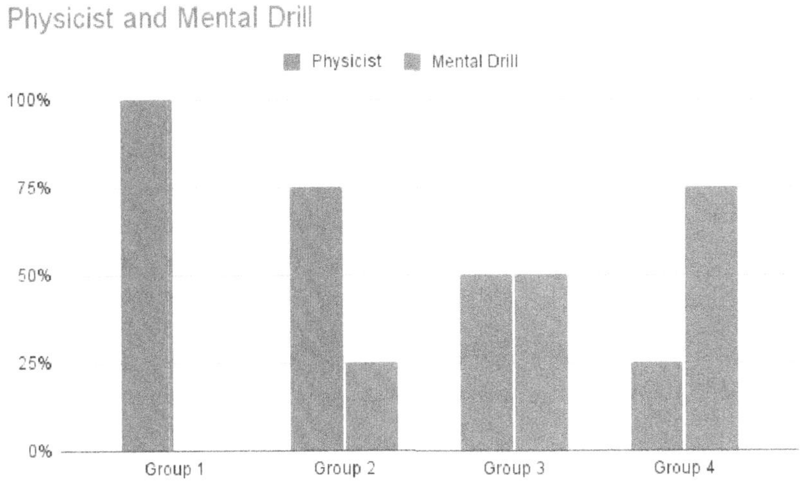

Guess which group had the best result? Group 4! Russian scientists discovered that visualization techniques stimulate a certain degree of physical movement. As the muscles remember the image of success, they keep daring for more as the athletes train Mentally. How does this relate to procrastination?

Visualization, Procrastination and Motivation

Are you not curious that all these three concepts have a common, "*ation*," which translates to "*action*". But that is not the only connection between the three elements though. If we allow these three activities to live intensely in our minds, we can reduce procrastination and achieve our goal, even if it's static procrastination. The human brain is not able to distinguish between reality and imagination. Remember the times you woke up sweating from nightmares? After all, it was not reality, but your brain had already ordered your body to sweat.

This brain characteristic may seem annoying sometimes but is valuable at other times. Imagining the details of the process of achieving your goal helps your brain value the action needed to perform the necessary action. You also get a small dose of motivation needed to defeat both static and dynamic procrastination. Let's get into more details.

Practical Visualization Technique for Motivation

When next you find yourself procrastinating and checking your Facebook profile or opening up electronics to read emails, just practice these three steps;

1. Go somewhere calm where you won't be disturbed. Close your eyes, concentrate on your breath, and count up to 30, rhyming with inhalation and exhalation.
2. Focus on your target with the details of the process that leads you to achieve that goal. Think of the goal in particular about what you see. What should you try? Add details of sound, smell, or anything you can tap.
3. Then, visualize the path that led you to your finish line. Which actions have you undertaken? Transfer the positive sensations related to your achievement to the process that helped you reach your goal.

That's it! Visualization should not exceed 5-10 minutes. Let your brain enjoy creative visualization. Within this time, you will get greater mental clarity, a pleasant feeling of serenity, and an awareness of what you have to do and everything that puts you to work immediately. Experiment with this technique daily, and you will begin to enjoy its benefits in one month without building yourself a particular room for meditation in your home. For me, most times, I run through these steps during my workout and gain motivation right from the beginning of the day.

We shall conclude this chapter with a small exercise.

Exercise of 10 whys

As I said earlier, one of the two ingredients of Motivation is "The secret is under your eyes" there are specific reasons that push you towards your goals and objectives. When we procrastinate, we often get involved in other activities that do not correspond to our *whys* for a purpose. It is mathematical that if we are unmotivated, we procrastinate. That is why I wrote this first chapter expressly on motivation. Even with the various techniques discussed, you still need to ask yourself one simple question before trying to change. Do I genuinely wish to achieve this objective?

If your answer is "no," it is useless to fight against the wind in the mills. This is because whether you choose to commit yourself today or tomorrow? You will still find yourself sabotaging your path. But if your answer is "yes," you have to recalibrate your motivation by finding out the "10 whys", which are the reasons that form your goal's base.

Write out 10 reasons why you want to reach your goal.

Because ______________________________

Because ______________________________

Because ______________________________

Because ______________________________

Because ____

Because ____

Because ____

Because ____

Because ____

Because ____

Wait! Did you complete the "10 why" exercise? If not, that would mean cheating, and I won't take it as a joke. Ignoring it means we will spend too much time helping your defeat procrastination. Get back to it.

Have you written your "10 whys"? Was it difficult? Since you have been true to yourself by writing down the 10 reasons why you are pursuing your objective. I am sure that you are already experiencing some motivation. That euphoric feeling that nothing can stop you. Well, that is precisely the time of emotion we need to pull the lever for a long-lasting action and push away procrastination.

With your presence in Chapter 2, I will see that you are now dedicated to taking action.

Chapter 4
Action

One of the lessons best lessons children learn through video games is standing still will get them killed quicker than anything else - Jinx Milea

Not doing the right thing at the right time, as you already know, is procrastination. So the major solution to it is taking action. If you are not going to get yourself, your dreams and visions, and your tomorrow killed, you have to take action. That is, quitting procrastination essentially means to start acting.

No matter how great the ideas you have are, if you fail to act, your life won't experience any change. This implies that only actions will change your life. Ideas never will. For example, having the thoughts that you will be a lawyer in the next ten years won't make you a lawyer if you don't take actions that will make you one. Going to school and studying is what will make you a lawyer. There is no how something that's only in your brain and not in your action cause change.

Before going to those actions we should take, we'll be talking about those 'frictions' that hinder you from taking action and induce you to procrastinate. Mistakes you shouldn't make if you want procrastination to go on extinction from your life.

Mistakes You Shouldn't Make

1. Promising: 5 minutes start

Think! How many times have you made these promises to yourself? "I'll do it tomorrow," "I'll go after lunch," "I'll read after seeing this movie." We postpone believing we will be more motivated in the future. But that's not always true. Most times, we'll always be who we are in the future we've set. That is, even after "lunch," after "tomorrow," nothing changes. Things remain the same as they've been.

When faced with a decision or a task to do, we usually rest on our self-control to push ourselves to get things done. Also, our motivation which is determined by the expectation of getting some reward for the work done, can give support to our self-control and make it more possible to do things in a timely manner. However, there are many demotivating factors that can be experienced that make us procrastinate easily. This 'promise to oneself' is one of them. It outweighs our motivation. Instead of doing what we ought to do at the right time, we do another thing and promise ourselves that we'll do it at a later time.

When a task asks for you to complete it, do it immediately. Don't ignore it. When you have the understanding that is promising yourself to complete a task that you ought to complete now in the future, you'll know that the best time to start is NOW.

2. Waiting till the conditions are right/perfect

Don't wait on perfect conditions for success to happen; just go ahead and do something - Dan Miller

Don't wait. Time will never be just right - Napoleon Hill

Do not wait until the conditions are perfect to begin. Beginning makes the conditions perfect - ALAN Cohen

Don't wait until everything is just right. It will never be perfect. There will always be challenges, obstacles, and less-than-perfect conditions. So what? Get started now. With each step you take, you will grow stronger and stronger, more and more skilled, more and more self-confident, and more and more successful - Mark Victor Hansen

Sitting on the sidelines and waiting for the perfect time to come is the biggest injustice you can do to yourself.

Most people think their present selves or the present situations or challenges are not able to perform certain tasks. They feel it's not the right time yet or set a criteria. For instance, "when I'm able to speak English fluently, I'll do the assignment," or "when I have more money, I'll start saving." They want to be perfect or do the task perfectly, without any mistakes or errors. (Most of them are perfectionists. This means that many procrastinators could be perfectionists).

Procrastination makes you think that your future self can handle a situation or task better than your present self. But in an actual sense, you'll never feel like you're in the correct mood to start and put an end to procrastination. Perfection is not possible to achieve, and aiming at it makes you have expectations that are not realistic. This could result in fear of failure - thinking 'doing it now' will lead to failure because the conditions are not perfect. Don't wait for perfect conditions, the perfect time when you cannot fail because it will never arrive. There can never be a perfect time to do something. Obstacles and hindrances are bound to come to play, so the right time is always 'now.'

The best thing to do is to start immediately instead of delaying or procrastinating. Be more deliberate about who you wish to be or what you wish to do. In other words, live in the present and not in the future. The more you wait to do something, the less likely it will be to do it. That waiting is creating steep resistance between you and the action you ought to do. Laziness, doubt, fear, then run to fill the space.

So just as it is essential for you to create the space needed to think rationally about the next right thing to do, it is also very important to act your way into what you want. You will be astonished by how much easier the task becomes once you start working.

If you feel intimidated or limited by certain things like beliefs, try to turn them into steps that you know you can do or achieve. Don't focus on doing everything if you start feeling you're not up to the task. Focus on taking one step at a time.

3. Researching your perfection

It is wrong to research your perfection before starting work. Fine, you could have a set goal, but that should not drive you to say it is either that or nothing. That is, if you don't do exactly like that, then it is a failure. That should not be. Moreover, you may never know how good you could be if you don't start. You may never get to know your strength or what you love doing if you don't start now. Those new things and styles in you, in your hands, may never see the light of the day if you refuse to start.

One of the reasons people procrastinate a lot is because they want to get the perfect outcome. They want to do something no one has ever done, the most superior, something that will be perceived as of the highest value. They dwell on the masterpiece of a task for a long time. "When I get the masterpiece, doing the work won't be difficult" - That's their language every time.

Pursuing perfection steals your time. It has the ability to kill your dreams and make it too late for you to do something important that you ought to do. It can result in burnout of very high levels, stress, workaholism, depression, anxiety, and so on.

The major reason behind the pursuit of perfection is the fear of failure. They are linked. You don't want to fail; that's why you fantasize about what you want the work to be like and how well it will be respected by people, and how high it will be rated. Since no one likes failures, we tend to fill our minds with thoughts of how we want it to be without getting our hands dirty. That is, without setting out to do the work. We postpone it to the future, which may never come. A seamstress or fashion designer who is afraid of cutting a piece of cloth wrongly may never bring out new styles in her if she refuses to start. If she keeps fantasizing about how the cloth will be when she finally sews it and does not get her hands to work, she will keep postponing till the end. This will even result in her disappointing customers and losing her integrity.

Whenever you find yourself fantasizing about making your masterpiece, just remember to get started. Do not waste your time thinking of the end product while doing nothing. Start now. Start writing the proposal now; stop thinking of how yours will be the best of all.

As important as making plans are, don't waste your time doing that and not working. You can not afford to plan for a whole lifetime and remain in the same spot.

4. Rationalizing the reasons for which you are postponing

Rationalization is making an attempt to explain or justify behaviours or attitudes that we know are not appropriate. It starts with a thought process that does not birth negative actions. This is a skill that is developed through childhood. It is talking ourselves into doing what we know is wrong using an excuse that we think is valid at the moment. It is convincing ourselves to procrastinate using valid excuses at the moment.

"I can't start writing now; I have a slight headache."

"I can't visit her today; I feel so tired. I'll go tomorrow."

"The project can wait. There's still time, and I even work better under pressure."

"It's okay to do the work later. It's still early; besides, productivity later in the day makes up for it."

Ignorance: "I didn't know I was supposed to do that."

"I don't know how to do it."

"No one really cares whether I do this or not."

"I need to be in the mood. I'm not."

"I know I can pull this out at the last minute."

"I just can't seem to get started."

"I just forgot."

These are just a few of the rationalizations we make when we postpone or procrastinate. We try to make our excuses rational, so we feel less guilty, making procrastination less bad than how it actually is. But doing this proves how much of enemies we are to ourselves.

As humans, we experience cognitive resonance, which is discomfort and anger when we do something wrong. So in order to decrease those feelings, we rationalize, trying to find the good reasons we did those things. The same thing happens when we procrastinate. We often feel very bad when we procrastinate, especially when it results in something very bad. But we try to find a valid excuse at that moment. Procrastination is a very bad thing in life, generally. But people rationalize it often to relieve the bad feeling that comes from doing it. The truth is that justifying our procrastination does not make it less reprehensible.

Rationalizing[9] our excuses cause us to be less accountable. We won't just be able to. And people will lose their trust in us. When we procrastinate instead of doing what we ought to do at the right time and then try to rationalize our excuses, people will expect less from us, and we gradually become insignificant. You don't want that. Do you? Even our lives generally will remain on a spot because those things that will cause us to move forward are swept aside for another time that may never come.

Always try to be solution-based. Do not try to rely on excuses. Be intentional about doing the right thing at the right time. Also, think less and work more. Understand that those rationalizations are bales, and for you to overcome procrastination, you must do away with them. Take action now. Take that step now. That's the only way to defeat procrastination.

5. Allowing Distractions

This is the last mistake that procrastinators make that we are going to be talking about. Distractions are major things that cause procrastination. Procrastinating does not mean you are doing nothing. It means you are leaving out the most important thing to do something that is less important or insignificant. That less important or insignificant thing is a distraction. Distractions are things that divert one's attention. For example, deciding to watch a movie instead of reading for an examination. One distraction, no matter how minimal, can send you down into the pit of procrastination.

Some of these distractions are:

Incoming emails- everyone has the mindset that every email needs to be responded to immediately. It's true, but it can be a very big distraction. If it is ok important, the sender will give you a call. Some-

9. Jacobs and Jerz (2017): How People Rationalize Procrastination

times, you just have to ignore the emails and do the right thing.

Overheard phone conversations- You have something very important to do, and you overhear your mum saying something to someone over the phone. It is familiar, right? That's a great distraction too. If you are not disciplined enough, you will find yourself procrastinating again and again.

Social media- This is one of the biggest distractions of this age. There is always something new that can take you away from your work- a consistent stream of new content that never comes to an end. Truly, it is not easy to avoid social media, but you have to try if you sincerely want to make a change in your life and community. You can switch off your phone, put it somewhere else, or do things that make you unable to access your social media accounts.

Listening to music- listening to music is good, especially when you are relaxing. But when you are doing demanding work, one where you have to do a lot of critical thinking or that you have to find out the best way to solve a problem, you have to do away with your headphones. It can hinder you from concentrating.

Always saying yes- Another form of distraction is saying yes at all times to all things or every request. Learn to say no to tasks and favours that won't add to your productivity. They keep you away from important things and make you set another time for the task. Ensure you evaluate the offers that come your way thoroughly. The best thing to do is turn them down- those offers that won't contribute to the achievement of your goals.

New ideas- Don't let new ideas take your attention away from what you are doing. You are working on something that is due in the next few hours. Then suddenly, you got new exciting ideas. It makes you think you are wasting your time doing nonsense which is not true. You want to develop those new ideas, so you put a pause on what you are doing. You will want to take a break before you start the new work. The best thing to do in this state is to write the idea or ideas on a piece of paper and go back to it later.

Most times, the distractions that come your way and get to you are caused by you. Try all your best possible to get rid of them and focus on the important thing. Doing this will impact your life positively.

Reducing Friction

Friction is like a sister to procrastination. Procrastination stands as friction between yourself and the goals you are to achieve. So the best way to get procrastination eliminated is to get the friction removed. Friction is like that thing that stops you from doing something right away. Let's say you want to make praying every time you come back from work a habit. But you noticed that the moment you step out of your car, people are always there to tell you one thing or the other (That's the friction). You can decide to pray before you get out of the car. You have to remove every friction point if you want to eliminate procrastination in your life. But before we go into ways to reduce friction, let's look at the causes of it.

1. The Distractions

Distraction is one of the, let's say greatest causes of procrastination. That's the main problem with distraction. When it comes, there will be very much difficulty in accomplishing a set goal. Sometimes, distractions can be real, like someone is at the door. That is, that distraction may be one good thing. And other times, it may be an activity that is not significant.

You may say you work better or give your best under pressure. Find out if working under pressure is really effective or if it's just procrastination in disguise. You may find out that you work better and produce better results when you are under less stress.

2. The Choices

Choices are fascinating, but having too much can make you paralyzed. Especially the fear of choosing wrongly that comes with it. But in this world, we have too many choices, leading to procrastination. Choices like so many paths one can follow career-wise, things to choose on the internet, and so on.

This present day is filled with so many choices that one puts off choosing one thing. We float on the sea of choices that we are not able to make a choice. Like saying you don't have clothes to wear when you have many of them staring at you in the wardrobe.

In the presence of multiple or numerous choices, it takes mental energy to make a choice. It is very much possible to put things off if they are based on our ability to choose. You will likely avoid making decisions when you can't choose.

3. The Difficulty

Another reason people procrastinate is the difficulty of the task when it seems too difficult. A person may keep postponing a task because he feels it is too difficult and he won't do it well. He may feel he is not equal to the task and continues avoiding it. He'll stay in his comfort zone, trapped there like a prison. He'll become so paralyzed that starting the task becomes a dream or, more so, a very high mountain. This will make him keep procrastinating.

Such a person will keep avoiding challenges that will help him grow. Challenges like building a relationship, pursuing your goals, and so on.

If you want to move forward, if you want to stop seeing things as impossible to do, you must learn to make the difficult easy. How do you do that? Learn not to see the task as a bug thing. See it as something you can do. Always tell yourself you can do it. Also, break down targets - take one step at a time. Don't always look at the end result. Break it into steps (achievable steps) and take each at a time. In other words, don't try to accomplish a goal at a goal, at once. Do it bit by bit.

Habits to Beat Procrastination

1. Reduce the number of decisions you need to make throughout the day

With every decision you make, you make use of energy. If you wake up in the morning and start asking yourself what you need to do, a great portion of your energy will be wasted thinking. And you'll eventually procrastinate because you won't be able to accomplish all that you decide to do. That's why you should reduce the number of decisions you make by making those decisions beforehand, before the breaking of that day. For example, pick the clothes you are to wear in the morning the night before so you won't have to waste time searching for the right clothes when you ought to be dressing up for the occasion. Doing this will make you save your energy to do the things that matter.

Give yourself rewards: Rewards, especially to yourself, are a good source of motivation. Promise yourself a treat after the success of every work or task. For instance, you can decide to buy yourself a drink after accomplishing a task. It will motivate you to do it.

2. Let others know about your goals

When you let other people, like your siblings, friends, colleagues, parents, etc., know about your goals, there is a very high possibility you will take it seriously and not procrastinate. This is because you know they will ask you about the goals, and it won't be nice, or you won't like to tell them you have not done anything about it. For example, if you are someone who writes stories on social media, you can let your readers know that you have started writing a new story so that you won't procrastinate since they are bound to ask you about it when they see that its release is delayed.

Give yourself a break: You might actually need a break. We are humans, and there are times we get tired and down. The best thing is to take a break. Don't try to continue with that task; else, the result won't be good. Don't be hard on yourself. You can even set a break time for yourself daily just to come out of maybe your daily routine. Have a time that you do nothing critical, just relaxing or playing, like sitting and observing nature. Just doing something out of that task.

Change your environment: Sometimes, procrastination is caused by one being in the wrong environment. Take a very good look at the place you are working. Does it make you want to work or sleep? If it always makes you want to sleep, then you have to change your work environment. Sometimes, the environment that makes you want to work before may not do that again. That implies that it is time to get your work environment changed. If you can't work well in a noisy place, then you know you ought to look for a quiet place to stay.

3. Remove your procrastination pit-stops

You procrastinating a lot may be a result of you making it easy to procrastinate. Take away those things that you know make it easy for you to procrastinate. Remove those distractions. You may decide not to check emails, track yourself, or get rid of social networks.

Move with those who inspire you to act: Identify those who inspire you to work, colleagues, or friends who trigger you to do the right thing. Move with them, hang out with them, and spend time with them instead of doing nothing or hanging out with those who will contribute nothing good to your life. When you do this, with time, you will see yourself inculcating their values or attitudes.

4. Break the task into little steps

The main reason some people procrastinate is that they see the task as too overwhelming for them. If that is the case for you, just break it down into steps and then focus[10] on one (the immediate step) at a time. You'll see that it becomes simple that you may even decide to do it now. Do the immediate step at a time without worrying about the next one. When you are done with it, then move to the next.

5. Create deadlines

After breaking your project into steps, the next thing to do is create deadlines for each step. When you do this, you know you are to complete a task on a specific date, and failing to do that may cause serious harm to your project. Don't make the mistake of setting just one deadline for the whole project. You invite procrastination when you do that. This is because you feel you still have time and keep postponing until it is too late.

10. Sam Chia (2021): Improve your focus and concentration: 15 ways to build your skills.

Chapter 5
Distraction = Destroy + Action

Seeing the topic, you may wonder where this is coming from. But it's the truth. If you think about it well, you will see that every time you give space to distraction, every time you give in to distraction, you are destroying an action. An important action you should have taken at a time will be destroyed because you chose to get distracted; you chose to postpone it. Therefore, distraction is the addition of 'destroy' and 'action.' In other words, distraction is the destruction of actions. Actions that would have gotten procrastination eliminated.

When you allow yourself to be distracted, your attention gets shifted. Then at some point, you have to shift it back to the right thing. You'd see that you are less productive because you would not be able to achieve or gain what you could have achieved or gained.

"Distractions destroy actions. If it's not moving you towards your purpose, leave it alone" - Jermaine Riley

Most times, distraction can be the result of not being able to pay attention or not being interested in the object of attention. Its sources can be internal or external. The internal include hunger, worry, or illness. External could include emails, phone calls, social media, and so on. The two sources are of great contribution to the interference of focus.

Distractions are like drugs in many ways. Just like drugs give immediate pleasure and deny one of long-term happiness and joy, distractions also give present pleasure and deny one of future happiness and joy. Also, just like drugs damage one's body, distractions damage the later time of the one who allows them.

All forms of distraction destroy actions. Some of them are ambient noise that hinders you from paying attention to the right thing, noisy equipment as a result of malfunction, rumination, use of cell phones, internet, social networks, gossip, and many more.

Valuable Actions to Destroy Distractions

Everyone has, in one way or the other, had to deal with times that come with the feelings of us being useless. Days that we get distracted while doing tedious and important work. To ignore distractions, destroy them, and improve productivity, there are actions we can take- valuable actions that destroy distractions. They include the following.

- **Dealing with emails expertly**

Emails can be so distracting that you forget you have any important task on your desk. But they are not something you can overlook or ignore. They are important too. That's why it's important they are handled expertly. How can that be done? Tools or applications like sandbox can be used. Apps like this notify you of only important emails that need to be attended to urgently. They also prevent spam from your inbox. They keep it clean and uncluttered. If it is impossible for you to use tools or apps like that, you can set a time to check your emails and get your inbox cleaned simultaneously.

- **Start small**

Some people have the mindset that productivity comes when you deal with big projects first. But that's not the case. Doing that can make you tired and burn out. It consumes greater energy, and so you may not be able to do any other thing. It's advisable to put smaller ones first. At the end of each, you will always have a feeling of accomplishment which will give you more energy or motivate you to do the next thing. Because knowing that you've accomplished something and crossing out done tasks on your to-do list is energizing. Getting to bigger tasks, you can now divide each up into smaller units. That will help you to go through them and get them done quickly.

- **Get help**

As much as self-discipline or internal discipline is of utmost importance, there can be limitations. We are humans, and humans will always have limitations. Sometimes, the reason we get distracted and procrastinate is that the work is too much for us. That way, you should get help from others. Tell others that can help with the project in your hands and ask them to render assistance to you. You are not an island, and you can never be. Those you tell can help you with it, motivate you, or advise you. Knowing that failing to do the right thing will not affect you alone but will have effects on someone else or others too will help you to destroy the distractions.

- **Be organized**

Lack of organization plays a major role in distraction and procrastination. Focusing on a messy desk is not easy or common. That's why your work area should be clean and organized. Distraction comes from having something undone at home, like an unclean house. When where you live is not organized, you may not be able to concentrate on why you are doing it. That is why it is very important to get the areas you live and work clean and tidy before you start that important project with you.

- **Media diet**

Smartphones and social media are very common when it comes to distractions. There will always be a stream of new things. If you decide to check just one thing before you know it, you are spending your precious time checking irrelevant posts. Shutting off the internet or even your phones can help here. This action can be of great value even while at work. You may think you can't do without social media, but that's not true. You try to shut off your activities for a few days and see if you won't live. Why should you allow others' lives to dictate how you live yours? You can freeze apps like Twitter, Facebook, Instagram, and other social networks for maybe a week (if they are your distractions) and see how much you will achieve.

- **Block time**

Switching between tasks makes it easy for one to be distracted. The best thing is to get your mind on one task at a time. Put the most important ones first and set a time for each of them since it takes focused time to do anything worthwhile. Be sure of why you want to do it and what you want to achieve (the expected result). Then set a specific time to get it done. Having a set time to complete a task will help you beat distractions as possible as much as possible.

- **Keep your goals and vision in mind**

To keep yourself from getting distracted, this is one of the things you can do. Keeping your mind on your goals and vision, what you intend to get. Know why you should not be distracted in the first place. Do you have a meeting to attend in the next few hours that you have to prepare a presentation? Do you have to submit a long essay tomorrow? Know why you should not be distracted and place your mind on it exactly.

- **Visualize yourself working**

Have the picture of you doing that work in your mind. For instance, a runner could imagine himself winning at first, then he acts the process backwards, starting from how he started the race before winning (in his imagination). A better way to do this is to imagine yourself doing a part of the work first and then doing it real before going to the next stage.

Imagine you want to wash a few clothes. You can start by picturing yourself rising from the bed where you are lying down. Do that, then picture yourself again picking the dirty clothes from where they are. Do that again and continue with the bit-by-bit picturing until you accomplish the task. Make sure you do all that you picture in your mind. And in no time, you will find yourself doing all you out to do at the right time without procrastinating.

- **Skip the unknown**

One of the things that open the door for distraction is battling with the unknown. When you spend a long time on a problem you encounter in a task, you may get distracted as a result of not getting the result quickly. It is possible you get tired of working, and something else takes your attention. You may become discouraged because the goal is a very big one, or you keep thinking of how you will feel or what it will be like to achieve the goal. That's why one of the things you can do in this situation to beat distraction is to skip whatever you don't know to return to it later. This implies that you should work on the easy part of the project first. Then come back to the parts that are more difficult. Hopefully, you may have gotten the solution, or you'll have enough time to think about it or even seek help.

- **Do the task as soon as possible**

Waiting can get you lost in distraction. The best thing is to start doing them immediately after you wake up. It's not easy, but waiting to do them can cause great harm. If you wait, distractions like unexpected calls and emails, a child you need to attend to, or even social media can gain your attention and you won't know when the time will pass you. Fine, you might have set a time to begin the task, but if you see that you are free before the set time, don't wait. Do it immediately. Don't wait till it is time because something else may come to play that you will forget you have something important to do.

- **Use a pair of headphones**

Using headphones, although seems insignificant, does magic. Even after doing away with all forms or sources of distraction, people around might still be a source of distraction. Using headphones helps to prevent the noise from the surroundings, either from people or things that get to you. It even gives a kind of gesture to people. It automatically tells people - DO NOT DISTURB.

Techniques For Maintaining Focus

One essential thing we could all use our time for is being able to focus. But one thing is to tell yourself to be focused and another thing is to be focused especially when the task is a mundane one. The former is easier than the latter.

Now, you are aware you need help. What are those techniques that can help you stay focused? You can decide to use one or all of the following.

- **Kill the distractions**

Do well to shut out both internal and external disturbances. There is no way you can be focused if you are bombarded with a lot of things. You are to concentrate fully on what you have to do presently. So you can start putting the distractions to death by doing simple things like blocking time in your schedule to perform an activity, closing the door to your office, requesting to be alone at that time, and leaving for a place where there is no possibility of noise. It can be a library, private room, or coffee shop. Applications and social media closed, notifications silenced and your phone out of sight. As the HBR described, it was found by researchers that when the phone is out of sight, cognitive capacity is significantly better.

- **Get enough sleep**

Lack of enough sleep is sure to deny you focus and concentration. Sleep is critical to our performance. A truth that cannot be denied or avoided is that as essential as food and water are, sleep also is undeniable, that even a little deficit can cause a big problem. Short and long-term memory, also the ability to focus, can be affected. As you know, you can't cheat nature. What is bound to happen will happen? Sleep is bound to happen, so it must. If you don't get enough sleep at night or after strenuous work, you won't be able to focus on whatever you want to do.

It is recommended for adults of ages 18 to 60 to have at least 7 hours amount of sleep every night, while adults that are older may need 9 hours of sleep every night.

Many things affect your sleep and one of the most common is reading from electronic devices like phones, computers, or tablets, or watching movies on TV or LED TV just before bedtime. Research has made us known that devices like that emit light towards the blue end of the spectrum. The light stimulates the eye retina and hinders the secretion of melatonin which works for the promotion of sleep anticipation in the brain. It is advisable to make use of a filter or blue light glasses to reduce the light. Or just avoid all electronic devices before bedtime.

There are many other ways to improve your sleep. They include: staying hydrated throughout the day, not exercising late in the day, making use of a bedtime routine and schedule that is predictable, engaging in breathing exercises, saying no to caffeinated beverages after lunchtime, and keeping the bedroom cool and quiet (an ideal temperature according to Cleveland Clinic is between 60 and 67°F which is same as 15.6 and 19.4°C). Another thing that can be done to improve the health of your sleep is to take time to wind down, that is, listening to soothing music, taking a warm bath, or reading a body.

- **Get your body fueled**

When hunger and anger come together to just one person, the focus will never be present. It is a focus fail. So for you to be focused, ensure your meals are not delayed or skipped. Your choice of food should be those that moderate blood sugar (vegetables, fruits, and foods that are high in fiber do this), fuel the brain, and energizes. Sugary foods and drinks should be reduced; those that birth spikes. They dip your sugar level and cause dizziness or drowsiness.

For your brain to function well, a lot of good fat is needed. Berries, nuts, coconut oil, and avocados are good sources. According to science, foods like blueberries can give concentration and memory boosts for up to 5 hours after consuming them. This results from an enzyme that stimulates blood and oxygen flow to the brain. It gives improvement to our memory and increases our ability to focus and learn new things.

Harvard medical school says a few of what is known as the best brain foods should be included for an extra boost. They include fatty fish like salmon, green and leafy vegetables like spinach, broccoli, kale, tea and coffee for the caffeine, in moderation, walnuts, berries such as strawberries, raspberries, blueberries, or blackberries.

- **Practice the Tomato technique**

Staying focused is not as easy as it sounds. But the Tomato technique can be of great help to you. So whenever you are battling with staying focused, try this technique. It is a time management method that Francesco Cirillo developed in the late 1980s. It makes use of a kitchen timer to break work into intervals, like 25 minutes in length. It is usually separated by short breaks.

This technique is good for you when you get derailed easily due to little distractions, enjoy gamified goal-setting, work past the point of optimal productivity consistently, when you like tomatoes, when you are too optimistic when it comes to how much work you can do in a day, and when you have a lot of open-ended work like researching for a blog post that can take a long time.

This method helps in training your brain to stay on an assignment for a short period of time. This is how it works:

- Pick a task
- Set a timer for 25 minutes
- Work on the task until the time is up
- Take a 5-minute break
- Every four tomatoes, take a longer 15 to 30-minute break.
- The 25-minute work sprints are the important part of the method, but the practice also involves three rules for enjoying each interval:

1. Complex projects should be broken down: If more than four tomatoes are required in a given task, it should be divided into smaller units. Doing this will help you to make recognizable progress.
2. **Small tasks should go together:** If there are tasks that won't take up to a tomato, they should be combined. For instance, "set vet appointment," "write rent check," and "read tomato article" can be put together in one session.

3. **A tomato must ring once it is set:** The tomato is a time unit that cannot be broken, especially not for checking things like text messages, incoming emails, or team chats. If those things come up, they should be taken note of and you come back to them later. Todoist, a digital task manager, can do this well, but pen and paper can also be used.

   If an unavoidable disruption occurs, you should take your five minutes and start again. It was recommended by Cirillo, who developed the tomato technique, that both internal and external interruptions should be tracked as they occur. Then reflect on how to avoid them in the coming session.
   The rule is applicable even if you finish your task before the timer goes off. You can make use of the rest of your time learning, getting skills improved, and for the scope of knowledge. For instance, you could make use of the extra time reading professional journals or researching opportunities.

4. **Be more mindful:** Distracted thinking is very common. So if you're experiencing it, you are not alone. However, it makes it difficult for us to maintain focus. This is where being mindful comes in. Mindfulness activities can make you more fit mentally and give strength to your well-being. It can also increase your ability to focus. During the activities, the brain experiences calmness and the whole body relaxes.

   Mindfulness means maintaining awareness of each moment where you are and doing what you are doing. Mindfulness helps you to understand or recognize the point where your attention shifts. Then you can bring your focus back to where it belongs, or where it is supposed to be, in no time. You can train your brain to be more mindful by putting into practice breathing techniques, mindful movements like yoga, and then meditation.
   During the process, you should focus on your breathing so that you will not be distracted. With regular practice, we will

be able to make use of our breath to bring back our attention to your current task so that it can be a success even if there is an interruption.

Choose to focus on the moment. You are in a position to choose where you put your mind or where you focus. It is not easy to concentrate when your mind is not in the present but in the past or even worrying about the future. It is tough, but you have to let go of past happenings. Recognize the impact, note what you felt and learned from it, then let it go.

Just like it, make an acknowledgement of your concerns about the future and how you feel about your anxieties, then decide to release them, and let them go. Get your mental resources trained in order to focus on the details of what is important presently. Our minds go wherever we choose to let it go.

5. **Engage in exercises:** Engage in simple exercises daily. Let your day start with it. The May 2013 issue of the Harvard Men's Health Watch showed us that when we exercise regularly, chemicals are released for mental sharpness and memory concentration. Other researches found that exercises can increase the brain's serotonin, dopamine, and norepinephrine levels. All these will have an effect on focus and attention. It is noticed that those who engage in regular exercises or sports perform better when it comes to cognitive tasks compared to those who do not. With physical exercises, muscles get relaxed, and the tension of the body is relieved. When the body is in good health, the mind also will be because the body and mind are closely linked.

Maintaining your focus[11] is not something you can achieve perfectly in a day. Even professional athletes need coaches so they can be focused and get the right move at the right time to achieve excellence.

11. Timothy J.Legg (2019): Need Help Staying Focused? Try These 10 Tips

The first step to take in order to maintain focus is to know how it is affecting you in all areas. For instance, you constantly get sidetracked by things that are not important. You don't go in the direction of what you aspire to; you struggle to meet appointments and commitments. Know that it is time to work on yourself. It is time to get help concentrating so that you focus better on things that matter.

Focusing is important for achieving success in academics, career, and life generally. By making use of the above techniques, you will accomplish more valuable things than before and be happy doing it because it is not just about doing things and accomplishing tasks but also making yourself happy and joyful so that your life can be meaningful and satisfying.

Chapter 6

FEWER ALTERNATIVES, MORE ACTIONS

As you begin this phase of taking legitimate actions to destroy your distractions, you may start to experience some delays in decision-making. This can be caused by many reasons, which include the excessiveness of options and choices. It is a situation where you have too many alternatives and options of what next step to take to achieve your goal. Even if you have the tasks spelt out in written form and pasted on the walls of your room, you will still subconsciously create options for other functions in the back of your mind, and these options will hinder your timeliness in taking the next step.

Often, these choices come up due to your worrying about the outcome of any step you take and the consequences. Coordinating your decision-making by streamlining your options and making them as few as possible will help you take more action towards achieving your goals. Although, some studies have proved that people like to have choices as it increases their motivation, control, task performance and even life happiness and satisfaction. But the real deal is that these studies presented people with just a few options and ever too many.

Options are like a representation of actions and a choice alternative. You have to choose between the represented activities by going through the imagination process. You take time to play the actions in your head and arrive at a result tagged as the consequence of the option or action. If you have laid out too many alternatives in your mind, then you have to play in your head and arrive at a conclusion. This is exhausting enough for any procrastinator to put off the task and forward it till tomorrow. We must scrutinize decision-making and eliminate alternatives to achieve progress and suppress procrastination for good.

The Consequences of overloading alternatives

Honestly, I have options not to write this book, to make it shorter, longer, wider, cheaper, or not write it at all. That's like too many alternatives, but I had to streamline them before they screw up my plans to get you out of procrastination for good.

According to[12] Barry Schwartz in his book, "*The Paradox of Choices- Why more is less,*" the vitality of choices on our fundamental. Well-being was well disclosed.

Schwartz made it so clear that having too many options can cause anxiety, dissatisfaction, stress, paralysis, and even bad decisions. We cannot ignore what we create daily. It never goes away from deciding which shoes to wear to what time to begin a task. Having too many options can cause the following;

- **Dangerous fantasies about better options**

When you have too many alternatives set before you, it is easy to imagine the ones that don't exist. You combine attractive features of existing alternatives to form more options for yourself. Instead of

12. Barry Schwartz (2004): *The Paradox of Choices'*

taking action, you get busy fantasizing and creating greater expectations. Your imaginations spread wide to the extent that it seems less satisfying when you eventually decide to choose an alternative. This is because you will always believe that other alternatives would have given you a better outcome.

- Bad Decisions and Regrets

With too many alternatives, decision-making comes with a trade-off of many options at an emotional cost. At a point, you begin to feel bad about choosing, and then you lose focus and get distracted from the concept of your decision. Hence, the result appears to be a result of making bad decisions, and you get enveloped with regrets about not picking other choices. All these negativities make even the most perfect decision become one that brings regret and dissatisfaction.

- Action Paralysis

In most cases, these negative feelings, fantasies and dissatisfaction often lead to being trapped in the result and fewer actions. Procrastinators will instead leave the actions hanging because of too many trade-offs or regrets from previous decisions taken. This situation is called action paralysis. You must have experienced it in everyday scenarios like choosing a shoe on the rack in a fashion store or deciding on a convenient savings plan. When paralysis sets in, it usually has a significant impact on the future because it drags in procrastination of decision-making.

The concept of Decision-Making

According to[13] Sheenar Iyengar, you make an average of 70 choices in a day. Social psychologies also emphasize that you make some options faster than others. While some scream, "*Pick me! Pick me!*" others get picked without a second thought. We need to make choices that will help us avoid procrastination, and understanding the complexity of decision-making is a good starting point. To choose wisely, you must perform these three mental tasks.

- Know what you want

This is similar to the awareness stage. When setting a goal, you must have figured out what you want and labelled them as your goal. So, let's say you want to organize a business webinar for colleagues at work and have alternatives of topics you want to discuss. In this case, the first question to ask yourself is, "*What do I want them to learn?*"

This streamlines the alternatives to the ones that relate to what you want. This is easy if you are trying to decide on an external course like the example above. But, in an internal situation, you will need to go through the self-assessment process to ensure you understand what you want. Having thoroughly digested the concept of self-awareness in chapter 2, I know that this will not be a challenging route to thread.

- Understand your options

Comparing and evaluating your options give you more confidence in whichever one you choose. But this will be brain-tasking if you have too many alternatives. If your options keep increasing, it may get to the point that you begin to think making a choice requires

13. Sheenar Iyengar (2010): *The Art of Choosing*

an expert of unique skill. This is the point where you imagine the scenarios attached to each alternative.

- Trade-off some available options

There are so many strategies for deciding which option to knock off to reduce the complexity of all your available alternatives. Two common strategies are *satisficing and elimination*. The satisficing approach involves considering the first option and never attempting to create more. It can be adopted at the initial stage of the decision-making process. Satisficing depends on the order in which you consider your options but should never be implemented with imagination to ensure that the choice will be the right one to support your goal. The fun thing is, even after creating a long list of alternatives, you can place them in order of hierarchy and adopt the elimination strategy for trade-offs. The elimination strategy involves ruling out options that don't meet the standard you have set for your goals.

The Theory of the Four Cs

Sheenar Iyengar believes that choosing problems occur nowadays because we have too many options, from picking an outfit to deciding on a savings plan. Hence, she, alongside other researchers, conducted a study on the retirement saving decision of about 800,000 Americans. They found out that the plans with more choices were less likely to be considered compared to plans with a few options. Also, even if these Americans pick a plan with multiple fund choices, they are less likely to choose the one that supports their interest in the long term. That means too many options led them to bad decisions or none at all.

With this well understood, Iyengar devised a technique to disentangle us from too many choices. Since having too many alternatives hinders your ability to take action, these techniques might work well in helping you cut options. I choose to call these the four Cs.

1. Cut

First, you must understand that less means more. The fewer your options, the more likely it is for you to get anything done at all. Resist the urge to create alternatives. Then, describe the differences between each of your alternatives, and then begin to eliminate the choices according to certain negativity they carry that might affect your overall result. This first stage is simply understanding your options which were earlier stated in the decision-making. Look out for redundant, extraneous, or choices that pose to have easily identifiable blockers and activities that are unrealistic with the situation you find yourself in.

2. Concretize

Here your imagination becomes concrete evidence or proof for success. Think about the outcome of the choices you have cut out. Consider the consequences and benefits of each of them. Then you will be able to access their usefulness in helping you achieve your goal. Your imaginations here must be vivid enough to concretize your goals. Iyengar added an exercise to the study for the employees that had not enrolled on any plan. She made them imagine the positive thing that would happen if they saved more. The exercise helped enrollment increase by about 20%.

3. Categorize

Group your alternatives to make it easier to choose. This categorizing will mean you have fewer alternatives. Arrange your options so those with similar needs and requirements fall under the same category. For instance, if you are planning to start a business, deciding on a location becomes a problem because you have multiple choices. You can group these areas according to the state's laws, financial requirements, sale benefits, etc. This will give you a clear view to choose which one best suit your goal. Any category you create must make sense to you as a chooser and not a choice-maker. So, do not be tempted to create more choices that fit into the category.

4. Condition

Your ability to make the right choices are determined by the conditions you place yourself. If you start with a few options and you have to create more along the way, you are more likely to make a choice that benefits your plan. On the contrary, if you have too many options, you can easily disengage, and in this course of procrastination, you are likely to keep stalling your next action. It is almost impossible to make wise decisions under choice overload. For the sake of your actions and mental health, be choosy about choosing.

Making choices affect every area of our lives. They are relevant in everything we do. Some choices affect our relationships, keeping us closer or farther away from our close friends. Other times we have to make choices that make routine a habit. Yea, procrastination is a choice, and you reading this book also means that you have chosen quick procrastination. As you begin to take action, reducing your alternatives is also a choice that will impact productivity. So being mindful of the consequences should never be neglected. Suppose you eventually make wrong decisions as a result of having too many options. In that case, your choice will impact your self-esteem, possibly reducing your interest in taking further actions and lowering your confidence.

Understanding the repercussions of making wrong decisions will prompt one habit that can further delay your ability to take action, including eliminating your choices. That is Overthinking.

The Overthinking Trap

At this stage of awareness, you become conscious of everything. Considering your failures in the past and the fear of failing in the future, you can get easily overwhelmed with thoughts of avoiding losses at all costs. You want to make the right decision and might end up losing sight of having a clear mind to worrying. This can slow down your mental process and make it too complex that decision-making becomes a hiding phase for more procrastination.

For instance, if you've been driving for a while, there is no doubt that you will make some complex decisions while driving without thinking too much. But for someone still learning, decision-making takes longer as the person tries to weigh out alternatives and their pros and cons. Even as a professional driver or expert, if you were to take a driving test again, you would be extremely conscious of your choices, no matter how small.

Examining all the components of your choices can be odd for your brain. It also slows down your performance and puts you in an uncoordinated state of confusion. You become in a state of worry, pressure, and continuous risk calculation.

I have advised that you streamline your alternatives, analyze the shortlisted options, and pick the best suit for your goal. However, there is a probability that you still fall into overthinking during this process. So, you need to get familiar with the signs of overthinking to know where to draw the line.

Signs that you are overthinking

- **Ignoring your Intuition**

Every time you are trying to make a decision, there is always an initial option that your mind agrees with. If you are an overthinker, you will have issues trusting yourself and agreeing with your mind's first choice. Then, you feel there is a need to stay longer in your thoughts and examine other alternatives critically. There is overthinking if you realize that you rely more on rational decisions than listening to the voice inside you. Learn to follow your instinct. Even if the option doesn't work, at least you have acted on it.

- **Afraid of wrong choices**

If you are always worried about making the wrong choices, no matter how little they are, you are overthinking things. The more people slow down decision-making to avoid mistakes, the more likely they are to make wrong choices. One of the reasons why you are afraid of bad decisions could be that you do not have enough information about the task. Hence, you pause on deciding to give yourself more room to acquire enough knowledge. But in most cases, it drags you down to overdoing research.

- **Researching options to death**

There is nothing wrong with researching well on your options, but when you have so much information than you need, there is a problem. If you are reading this and currently thinking of taking a course or certification in decision-making to reduce your alternatives, you are already overthinking. An overthinker would be willing to acquire degrees and additional certification on the next steps before making a choice. Without a doubt, as a procrastinator, you will still put off research until tomorrow.

- **Obsession about things beyond your control**

Your future is beyond your control, so when you plan, leave it and let things play out. Don't get too obsessed with making things work; else, you will build anxiety and start getting delicate about every affair. This will cause you to focus on your options instead of taking action.

Overthinking prevents progress as you get trapped in your thoughts and become less confident about taking action towards achieving your goal. It becomes difficult for you to separate facts from fallacies because of the fear you have created in yourself. The fear will make you judge yourself harshly and doubt your abilities. As you know, beginning action with this level of negativity hinders your ability to succeed.

Dear overthinker, it is time to get out of the trap. If you aren't in it yet, you must understand the signs listed earlier and know when to quit so you don't end up hurting.

Overcoming the Overthinking Trap

Overthinking is exhausting, and if you want to get yourself back on track, you must find a way to regain perspective. Look at it this way, you are supposed to be creating solutions to your challenges, but when you overthink. You seem to be making more problems that can keep you under your challenges for as long as possible. I have some strategies from the[14] metacognitive theories that can help you get over this thinking problem and get back on track.

First, ask yourself, "*Is this helping?*", "*Can I come up with actions in this situation?*" Find awareness and be sure that you are overthinking. That is why you have those signs listed up there to help you figure out your thinking status. Remind yourself that this is a cycle of more problems, and it is not helping. Consider how much harm the situation has caused you and how much time and energy you have lost trying to get more and more resources for your choices.

Overthinking starts with a trigger thought. After you figure out that you are overthinking, you need to find the trigger thought. 3 Researchers have estimated that humans produce thousands of different thoughts and memories every single day. Most of these thoughts go unnoticed, while some stick around and attract our attention longer than others. The longer you stay with these thoughts, the more you get some associated sensations and feelings, and they won't just fade off easily.

Trigger thoughts may and may not be harmful. It depends on the emotions associated with them. For example, if you have thought about an upcoming book launch or a meeting with a friend and you become excited and look forward to that day, that is not harmful.

14. Julie Tseng, Jordan Poppenk (2020): Brain meta-state transitions demarcate thoughts across task context exposing the mental noise of trait neuroticism

But you must stop when the thought is clouded with so many "*what ifs..., whys, and hows*" that eventually become worries.

Your thoughts are like trains on the railway; you can't jump on every train that passes, so you must learn to let your trigger thoughts go instead of developing and multiplying them. The more you engage in trigger thought, the longer it takes to take action. Once you can put off negative trigger thoughts, you will become lighter and faster with decision-making.

Understanding your trigger thoughts, you should learn to pick out what you can and can't control. Though you don't have control over the trains that come your way, you can choose to board or not. This also applies to trigger thoughts. You cannot control which thought creeps in, but you can choose which ones to nurture or answer. As I mentioned, ideas come in thousands every day. You may not remember the thoughts of yesterday unless you have chosen to begin a conversation with them. When you get a trigger thought, and it's likely to make you overthink, you can choose to ignore and postpone your worries to reduce them. That is how you control your thoughts.

Overthinkers have challenges believing that they can control their thoughts. One easy way to reduce or postpone worrying is by giving it a specific time of the day, like 8:00 pm. So, if any idea you wish to develop comes in, then you can simply deal with it later at the appointed worrying time. With this, you get to reduce the time you spend worrying daily and do more actions. You can now challenge the thought that you can't control your worries.

Also, thoughts that creep in during the day will seem less important or problematic later in the day. Setting a worrying time will help filter essential issues like planning your task or achieving your goal. For instance, you have a problem creating an outline for your following thesis. While you start your day, many options start creeping into your mind. As you note the list of topics to include in the thesis, you get stuck deciding between a similar list of ideas. The best thinking is to take a pause and revisit the decision at your worry time. When you review the thought later, some options will begin to appear less important than the others and save you more thinking time. You can now easily decide which ones to go for. Meanwhile, if you choose to solve that problem instantly as the thoughts come, you will most likely conduct extensive research on every option. Very exhausting!

Postponing your thoughts till the appointed time will be easier if you shut them down with a little distraction. Look for activities that you enjoy most and maximize them at that moment to avoid the urge to overthink. Push off negative thoughts. That's the only procrastination I support. Negative thoughts always come with fear or anger, so you can't miss them.

Choice overload is a common reason for overthinking and a soft-landing excuse to procrastinate. The longer it takes to decide which options to take, the more likely you are to procrastinate. So, if you have postponed the thought of choosing your worry time and you still have choice paralysis, put yourself under time pressure. Add a deadline to this decision or the action. One sweet strategy that would work here is to set a timer for decision-making. You then fall under pressure as you see the clock ticking.

Finally, eliminating choices means taking the bull of procrastination by the horn and living by your own rules. Choose the thoughts that matter to you to avoid overthinking. Add time pressure to decide faster. Don't let fear take charge of your thoughts. Rise from your choice paralysis by trusting your instinct more.

If choosing is not a challenge for you at the moment, another common blocker is handling difficulties. Trust me; I've got techniques to sort this out in the next chapter.

Chapter 7
Making Difficulties Easy

Procrastination occurs for many reasons, most of which are unique to the procrastinator; hence we cannot exhaust these reasons here, but we have to deal with some most common causes in the previous chapter. So, what if alternatives and decision-making are not a problem for you? Then, you may be facing something more complicated. When I was still a chronic procrastinator, I emphasized every difficulty I perceived in a task, no matter how little. It becomes an excuse for me to skip the task till the next day, which can go on and on for weeks and months.

Trust me, postponing your task because of little blockers is almost irresistible. First, have the result in mind and let it motivate you toward overstepping boundaries. With the goal in mind, you can avoid obstacles and solve problems that seem to hinder your progress. However, you may face some real difficulties that make your plan seem unachievable. For instance, when you get a massive project to manage, it seems to be beyond you.

For projects that are enormous and time-consuming, postponing is a dangerous game. Most times, you will end up rushing things towards your deadline. This eventually leads to the dangers of procrastination, which include total failure or unproductivity. Breaking your large projects into the smallest unit of tasks is the best approach to getting them done without slacking. I recommend the

Work Breakdown Structure (WBS) as the most relatable strategy for making difficulties easy.

Besides WBS being a foundation for project management, it is also a perfect tool for combatting any urge to procrastinate. This concept is as old as time and very relatable.

Let's begin...

The Concept of WBS

Work Breakdown Structure was initially introduced by the U.S. Department of Defense while developing the missile system as far back as the mid-1960s. They used this concept in planning and controlling large acquisition projects with the objectives of developing and delivering weapons. Contractors were given different responsibilities and managed by a central administrative office. The concept was used to ensure that the total project, no matter how large, was thoroughly planned ad organized to ensure successful completion and commendable deliveries. Don't worry. We aren't using the WBS to plan any World War except the war against procrastination.

Let's get serious.

Work Breakdown structure is a great tool used to manage the most critical projects. It simply breaks work into smaller tasks to make them manageable and approachable. Most companies use WBS for every project to track progress and ensure they reach their goals. You can use this to get the best result in everything you do. The structure provides a solid foundation and guideline to success as it itemizes unique tasks, essential elements, and milestones of a project and places them in a hierarchical structure that helps you see any large project in small bits.

According to the Project Management Institute (PMI) Project Management Book of Knowledge (PMBOK) WBS is defined as a "deliverable oriented hierarchical decomposition of the work to be executed by the project team to accomplish the project objectives and create the required deliverables. It organizes and defines the total scope of the project. Each descending level represents an increasingly detailed definition of the project work." This ascertains that discipline and determination are all you need to achieve the best result when using WBS. Most project managers use the WBS Structure. Why would you need this if you are not one?

To Boost Productivity

Procrastination impedes your productivity. As you face more difficulties in projects you have to handle, the tendency to procrastinate increases. The Work Breakdown Structure helps you identify specific skills that will make your work faster. It enables you to figure out strategies that will improve your productivity. It becomes easier to identify the tools needed to get the job done. This, in turn, results in a well-organized execution and completion of the project. Honestly, that is something you can't get from overthinking strategies or procrastinating until you are convinced you can handle the task.

Improve Transparency and Accountability

WBS helps you provide every detail you need to commence the project to the lowest level. It gives you a head start that helps you a clear transition into success. If you will be working with a team. It helps you get a better understanding of every member and their responsibility. WBS gives you a transparent breakdown of how you can achieve your objectives with success. It also helps to record your process, steps, challenges, and success. This makes it easy to detect errors and flaws that will help future recommendations.

Allocate Cost and Time

Cost and time are always highly considered in every project, and they can also determine the success or failure of projects. So, vividly itemizing the cost of every procedure and how long it will take will help in project management. With WBS, you can estimate the time it will take to complete each task in the project. This estimation will create deadline pressure at every project stage and help you avoid procrastination and overthinking. WBS also enables you to generate cost estimations that reduce your ability to make too many alternatives, which could slow down your actions.

Easily Identify Risks

WBS brings clarity, and that will definitely help you figure out challenges and risks in your project flow. You can quickly identify threats ahead and reduce their chances. Identifying risks does not mean that they are entirely eliminated. It just means that they can be avoided or the dangers reduced.

Close monitoring boosts progress.

A breakdown structure of work has been broken down into easily identifiable deliverables that can be used to measure success. You can also quickly figure out delays caused by sub-deliverables. The faster you identify uncertainties, the quicker you get rid of them, and the easier it is to meet deadlines. WBS allows you closely monitor every bit of the project so that you can take faster and safer actions to avoid risks and build success.

Despite the many benefits of the Work Breakdown Structure, there are still some disadvantages, especially that of the step-by-step approach. It could be stressful to make a long to-do list, but that is also the simplest thing to do to make any difficult task easy. But you can split the entire project into phases and then work on the checklist as the phases begin. If you aren't strategic enough when using WBS, you might have too many tasks to do at once and feel overburdened.

Types of WBS

There are two types of Work Breakdown Structure, and your choice depends on whether you want to divide your project according to time or scope. They include 1) Deliverable-Based and 2) Phase Based. However, the most common one is the Deliverable-based approach. What differentiates the two types of WBS are just the elements identified in the first level.

Deliverable-Based Work

As the name suggests, the deliverable-based WBS portrays the relationship between the project deliverables and the scope. It shows all the significant areas of the project as control accounts and divides them into deliverables and work packages. It helps you know how the different items needed to complete the project relate to one another. They also provide a natural summary of the entire work to varying levels with accuracy to cost and resource estimations. An example is a contractor breaking down the scope of his project based on the physical locations of the different components. His WBS will show all he has to deliver in those areas, what he needs to get the job done and maybe what defines the work's success.

Phase-Based Work

Here the WBS shows the final deliverables at the top of the chart and the different levels of the work-based structure (initial, planning, execution, control and closeout) below the deliverables. It focuses on what should be done to arrive at a completed phase. It provides a more thorough breakdown of the work and secures high-quality deliverables. It also defines the different disciplines needed to get a job done. The elements of the structure are usually provided in a hierarchical structure that shows the breakdown of steps.

One most important things is to have a suitable structure for any project, including selecting the correct elements and placing them at the right level. As we dive deeper into the Work Breakdown Structure, you will understand the different levels of the structure and how to apply it in whatever project gets you stuck in procrastination.

A good structure must be well-defined and easily understood. It should also show the task durations, cost and resources required, irrespective of the type of structure you choose. You should also see specific responsibilities assigned to make the project easy to manage. If you are working alone, you must spell out your task clearly enough. Consider making sure that every task listed is its lowest breakdown. Write them in tiny bits of tasks. All the start dates and completion dates should be assessable at every milestone.

Levels of Work Breakdown Structure

In previous paragraphs, I have introduced you to the levels in the work breakdown structure. Understanding the levels deeper is essential, and learning how it helps you achieve your goals. The WBS levels help you prioritize and organize your tasks based on what needs to be completed before achieving success in others. There are four WBS levels.

The Top Level

This contains the title of the project and its final deliverables. It helps you see the overall scope of the project. You should start with clear language that states the expectation at the end of the project and what it should look like to everyone. It is a simple way to give yourself that assurance that this is not as difficult as it seems. This top-level can also serve as a motivation throughout the project. Write it in a way that sets your mind clearly on the goal. For example, if the project is your first Brand Design project. Let the top level clearly state that. And if it is a project that leads to your promotion at work, let it clearly say that. Regular project managers might just have to state the topic. But in the case of procrastination, remember you need to keep your motivation close to your heart at all times, so state the achievement attached to your project at the top level of the chart. Out of sight might indeed mean out of mind if you do otherwise.

The Control Account

Next, list the control account of your Work Breakdown Structure under the top level. On this level, you outline the different phases of the project and the key things that should be delivered. It also includes significant parts and features that need to meet expectations upon project delivery. At this stage, you just highlight all the requirements your project has to meet. For instance, if you are to organize a seminar for your company. The phases will include acquisition of audience and speakers, creatives and marketing, Welfarism, and follow-up and report in your control accounts. You will be accounting for these stages to state that your seminar was successful entirely. Another example is when you have to do some software developments, the main components like database system, search function, chat features and the likes will be categorized at the control accounts level of your Work Breakdown Structure.

Work Packages

Here, the total breakdown of the control accounts is listed. It appears below the control accounts and gives a minor breakdown of the deliverables under the control accounts. These are tasks that need to be completed before you can deliver success at the control accounts level. For example, the database systems in the control accounts level of your software development projects will not be successful without some tasks. You need to develop the application, servers, data structure, and others at the work packages level. For this level, create a new list of individual tasks for each control account. This helps you stay organized and on schedule. Adding timelines to these task lists will be very beneficial to the timeliness of delivering the entire project.

Activities

This is the last stage where all the tiniest tasks are listed. It contains everything you need to execute the work package level. Nothing is too small to be listed here. If you have time and cost indicated at the work package level, you must also break it down along with the activities to avoid slacking. This simply shows that to develop the application at the work package level, you must configure and install a database or integrate a server. These are the smallest activity for each task. It helps to improve productivity and ensure that no significant or minor task is left undone. These levels allow you to see your progress towards achieving your goal from the smallest unit.

Understanding the different milestones and how to set them accurately is necessary. Other formats used in the work breakdown structure include the tree format, outline format, hierarchical structure, or tabular structure. It depends on what you find suitable and what fits your needs. Remember that you are trying to fight procrastination. Hence, you must choose a format that is easy to construct and follow. Try to eradicate every excuse that can hinder your creation of a WBS. You can also use specific software to ensure you have the proper structure and reduce clumsiness.

However, there are specific rules to follow to achieve an effective WBS. This project decomposition can be done in stages, on processes, or by location, all of which are targeted towards success. Each level must be clearly defined to avoid duplication of tasks or work.

The 100% rule of WBS

A basic 100% rule guides the creation of a WBS and states that a WBS must contain 100% of the work needed to complete the project. All the necessary aspects, both internally and externally, and contracts must be represented, including the full management of the project. This means that everything is an important detail. Nothing should be omitted. The rule applies to all levels of the work breakdown structure. The entire 100% of the work packages for the control account must be represented, and all the activities for the tasks under the work packages.

I know all these might seem a little complicated, so here are some tips you should apply to make your organization accurate.

- **Define your Scope, Goals, and Objectives**

We really can't do anything without setting our goals and objectives in line with motivation. Defining your goals and objectives gives you clarity on the path you must tread to get there. For example, if you have been assigned a large marketing campaign. The campaign's goals and objectives must be well stated to help you fully understand the right strategies and approach to take towards the campaign's success. These set-down dreams and goals will also be a source of motivation if the process ever becomes too tiresome or challenging, especially for procrastinators.

- **Identifying Project Phases**

As you have fully defined your scope and goals, you break them into a series of phrases. Create a control account showing the category of the different tasks you will perform. With this, you can calculate your success and keep track of the status of your work. If decomposition seems complicated at this point, do a little research on the project and see if any available WBS templates can help you get a clearer picture of what the control accounts must contain. Again, this must be 100%.

- **Set deliverables**

A deliverable is everything you need to do to be successful at every level of the WBS.

These deliverables are also crucial things that determine the entire project's success. You must break them down systematically and accurately. Make sure you reach every single task and have it documented, no matter how little. These should include budget resources, milestones, and deadlines that are suitable for thc task. Working with a group, you may also choose to split the breakdown according to the role and individual tasks. There is no limit to the number of tasks to be listed.

- **Prioritize dependencies**

Some tasks solely depend on one another. You must consider this when listing. Map out these dependencies, as they can help you identify and manage risks and challenges. It also allows you to stay organized throughout the project. Just imagine placing a website developer placing website design over buying a domain. There must be a smooth flow of tasks to reduce delays.

- **Set Deadlines**

Deadlines should be added at all levels of your WBS. It helps to create proper time management. Use a deadline to determine the overall duration of the project. For projects with deadlines, use deadlines to speed up delivery without a last-minute rush. This is a perfect tool for any procrastinator. Even if you have struggled with postponing, you will have a deadline rush at every task or level. However, you still need your ability to stop procrastination and discipline from being religious with timelines at this point.

- **Track Progress**

Understand all the Key performance indicators attached to every task. This way, you can measure their progress and success, improve productivity, and identify areas of improvement and difficulties. There must be close markings and monitoring of the Work Breakdown Structure. The earlier you identify a slack, the easier it is to eliminate it. Also, tracking progress will add more wings to motivate your actions towards completing the work.

5. Write Notes

Include short descriptions and comments at every level or task. You can use this to recount the experience, including blockers and recommendations. This comes in handy when you are writing your reports at the end of the project. It also makes it easy to address anything that doesn't quite fit into the structure or anything that must be added.

1. Be Thorough

Nothing is too small to be done. Take every little task with complete seriousness. They are like little holes that can widen and swallow the entire project. List out everything, big or small.

It's been a long read on Work Breakdown Structure. It's a large scope, and we cannot complete it all in this chapter. But, I believe you have picked up tips to help break the difficulty and make your project easier. I imagine you have this all drawn out in your head already. As much as you use a pen and paper to make this work, I suggest you try out WBS Software that you will find online. This will add speed to the completion of the structure. You are already a procrastinator; anything that seems like a task will always look up to you for some postponing. Don't yield to their puppy eyes.

Since you are still reading up to this time, I am sure you have broken the procrastination barrier. We are gradually heading to how this can work if you try one tip to avoid procrastination once a week. Remember, Rome wasn't built in a day and cannot be destroyed in a day. The next chapter is about you getting free from this spell of procrastination. There is a truckload of liberating activities waiting for you to read them.

Chapter 8
Liberating Activities

In previous chapters, I have suggested several habits that can contribute to helping you quit procrastination. There have been lots of tips and scenarios. It is time for us to go straight into how these habits can be lined up as a practical solution to your procrastination problems. I have ten liberating activities for your transmission. But just like I had mentioned, nothing works on its own without effort and determination. The world doesn't change on its own. Act more and stay true to your commitments. There is no better time to start than yesterday.

Let's talk about the 10;

1. Magic Phrase

You know how magic feels like "wow", like more enlightening, like bright eyes, a huge smile, and every expression showing that you are aware. That's it. I want you to pick your triggers and understand them so well that when you experience them, you will be lightened up. Know what leads to your procrastination. When an action is about to be taken, there are two things to expect. It is either result or an excuse. For procrastinators, excuses are most common and not hard to find. When little things become a reason to ignore your task, you are making up excuses.

Watch out for thoughts like "I can't deal with this right now," "I don't feel like doing it today," "I work better when the deadline is close," and "It's not that hard. I will do it later", "I don't really understand." Write the date and time in a notebook. Most reactions to these thoughts will be a conclusion to skip the task. Fight that off. Look for immediate solutions to these excuses. If you don't understand the task, do more research. If you don't feel like doing it today, that's the next time. Kicking the butts of excuses officially helps to guarantee a better result. Take note of every magic phase you have daily. That equals the number of chances you have to fight procrastination. Keep your mind enlightened about these excuses and reduce the chances of falling into them again.

You can have your friends help you out here. Honestly, there will still be the temptation to skip this magic phase until the next action. Well, it seems like a speedy recovery, but eventually, you will realize that you have missed activities at certain unidentifiable times. This awareness stage is the most important part of the process. Once the excuses are written down, the next time you feel them, they will be weightless and not strong enough to make you skip your task. The reason becomes magically invalid. Don't get it twisted. Writing down the excuses is not enough to make it go away. You still need to put in determination and effort.

2. Create moments of idleness all-day

One season you might be procrastinating a particular task because you feel exhausted from the day's activity. This exhaustion can lead to postponing your task until the next day. However, you can ease the hard work by creating little time to rest and stay idle. If you live every day with too much concern and distress about your commitments, you need some moment of idleness. Dedicate a minimum of 15 minutes to a maximum of 60, too, so some fun activities will help you relax your mind. Try reading, movies, meditation, music, or sports. With activities like this, you can recharge your thoughts. This deliberate procrastination will help you reboot your thinking and refresh well to continue your task effectively without hitting a block. Yes, it's positive procrastination, but it must not be overused. Never let this moment of idleness come after thoughts like "I will do it later" or "This is overwhelming." It should be a *dedicated* time frame recurring every day and simultaneously. This is a break for results and not a break because of excuses.

According to an organizational psychologist, researcher and New York Times bestselling author, Tasha Eurich, "*Even though we try to fill up every moment, modern life is punctuated by lulls. Take advantage of opportunities to turn your brain off during your commute, at the gym, or while waiting for a tardy lunch date.*"

Taking a break from things will help your brain stay healthier, and you can uncover ideas that have been hidden in your unconsciousness. A little bit of Idleness gives you a happier, healthier, more creative brain. Even if you need to be punctual at your deliverables, find time every day `to turn your brain off. You can also schedule that little time to leave your work area into a more comfortable zone, setting you in the mood to relax and refresh. Idleness doesn't just happen. You have to plan it and stay committed. It is not the same as laziness. You are not avoiding putting your effort to work. You are simply taking a little break. Time is idleness, and if you want to stay dedicated to your moment of inactivity, you must respect time. Too much time wasted idling will have negative rather than positive. That will be one huge procrastination problem starting up again.

3. Act Despite Everything

There is no better time to start acting on your tasks than yesterday. I say 'yesterday' because you could have done the task but postponed it. You can never be ready enough, so you must act despite challenges. Motivate yourself to tackle any action that makes you uncomfortable at least once a day. In your to-do list, there are certain activities that you are always motivated to do, and there are some others that seem not to interest you for specific reasons. That's the deal. Act on them no matter what. There is no perfect time to be ready or confident to do anything. Just act. Make it another daily task to perform on any task that makes you uncomfortable. No action is too big to be tackled. Do not let the urge to postpone your task take control.

Always hold on to whatever motivates you. These motivations are motives for your actions, so they will comfort you whenever it seems complicated. The rules are simple, and the steps to take are not hard. You already know that to stop procrastination, you must set your goals which will stand as motivation, identify the problem and be aware of whatever makes you postpone, then create a plan of action. After completing this plan, break them into smaller tasks, prioritize them and create a routine.

Sometimes even after doing all these things, you will still find some smaller tasks that feel uncomfortable. This is where those goals you set at the initial stage become very useful. They help you act despite everything. Use the deadlines you have put in your action plan to create pressure to instigate more actions. Though rushing to complete a task before the deadline might not always yield the expected result, it still works well in helping you complete your task without procrastinating. Another strategy is to change your mindset. Stop subjecting your identity to that of a procrastinator. Suppress thoughts like, "I can't do this now," "this must be later," and other procrastination triggers with actions that take the task off the list and also the procrastination out of the picture. Just Do it and cross it out of the list.

4. Avoid the trap of results.

Yeah, we are back at it. The trap of results can make you paranoid, worried, and stuck. It is that urge to see effects happen as fast as possible. You expect everything to happen right away. Expect hurdles along the line, and don't think growth is linear. Setting high expectations for anything you do is normal, but you must also learn to appreciate the small wins. Stop judging your result. Do this on the list for one day a week. Procrastination has made you waste so many days of your life. Now that we need to stop this habit. Try sacrificing just one day every week to stay clean. Choose one day to commit to your decision. Wake up early, follow your diet, meditate, and practice everything you would have postponed.

Make sure that you are not keen on seeing the result urgently. For instance, if you are trying to lose weight and start a diet and exercise. A psychological effect makes you want to see changes right from the next day. Meanwhile, change comes gradually, and at the initial stage, there is a tiny result that you can't see. Then, you can easily lose motivation and reduce action because you have been disappointed by your progress.

Use the chain or climbing strategy to record your progress, no matter how little. Then, you will see the significance of every action you take towards achieving your goal. Calculate progress bit by bit because the result combines all your progress at different activity levels. Your progress chain motivates you to continue until you have met your target. So, instead of waiting for a drastic shed of weight, you can hop on a weighing scale every morning and write down how tiny a difference you have from following the dieting and exercise procedure thoroughly the previous day.

If you let yourself get discouraged by the trap of results, you will lose your focus on your goal and dwell in the worry of how you have failed at getting the job done. Do not be too hard on yourself. Even in the case of fighting procrastination, changes will only come gradually. Set your expectation on the little progress you can see and celebrate it. Small wins are a tiny part of big wins in creation.

5. Use Creative Visualization

Motivation to take action usually comes from a correct perception of reality. This is typically explainable by the common saying, "*Seeing is believing.*" Think about the outcome of the actions you have planned. What do you want to achieve? For instance, if you have a large project at hand with a promotion as a reward. Have a visualization of what it would feel like to be in a higher position or at a senior level of your career. Imagine the process and actions you took to get to the endpoint.

Use the power of imagination to get what you want. Form a vivid mental image to change your thoughts and beliefs. This technique was often used to create psychological changes like pain reduction and wound healing. It is also an effective way to improve your confidence and productivity. But whatever you imagine must be realistic and achievable. That is what makes it a perception of reality. Think through the path you have to thread to get to your imagined outcome. Spend 10 minutes of your time daily to imagine yourself reaching your goals.

Remember the emphasis on "*correct perception of reality.* There is no luck or magic attached to creative visualization. Though it is an image, it should be as real as possible. Avoid creating fallacies and think of what is true. Choose a goal you can meet and set smaller goals that act like stepping stones to the primary goal. These smaller goals are actions that are required to set you on the path to success. Form a mental image of the outcome and make it look like it already exists. Picture the image with positivity and imagine how you overcame challenges along the way. Have this imagery in your head daily, and see how your life gradually transforms into being the achiever in your visualization.

Creative visualization must be used with an open mind. Picturing it doesn't mean that is precisely how it will turn out. Stand on the possibility that it might work, and you must not underestimate the need to keep your hopes up. Create a balance and guard your feelings to avoid disappointments. Practice visualization while you are meditating or relaxing. Make it a practice and maintain consistency. It is a huge tool for becoming a better person.

6. Start a media diet

We have analyzed how distractions influence our tendency to procrastinate. One major factor of distraction is technology and media. They make us victims of procrastination faster than any other form of distraction. You will agree that there are many times you neglect your tasks to watch videos and memes on social media. Before you know it, you have spent almost all day strolling from one app to another and one video to another. Then, you get exhausted and postpone your task to tomorrow. Sometimes it gets as bad as you keep refreshing social media platforms to catch the latest gist as it drops.

The more time you spend on Facebook, Instagram, Twitter, or TV programs, the more you suffer from unproductivity and delays.

Even if social media and other media channels pose a benefit by our keeping us engaged with the outside world, they can still keep you out of the world. Start a strict media diet for one day a week. Pick a day of the week when you will not use any media channel. For one day, eliminate Facebook, Instagram, TikTok, Twitter, online news, Tv programs, and other social networks completely.

There are two likely reasons why you procrastinate on social media. Sometimes you turn to social media when something pushes you to postpone your task, or you just choose to ignore it in the meantime. Then, you turn to social media to keep yourself busy for that period. Another way you can procrastinate with social media is when you allow it to distract you from your task until you procrastinate. For instance, you are currently trying to study for a project, and your phone notification keeps beeping with updates from social media. After checking the notification, you find yourself scampering these social platforms until you finally abandon your study and focus on gathering delight from social media platforms.

Stop the distraction as quickly as you can. It may seem hard for you now, but it's not too much to give up for one day.

Think of how much this distraction is making you give up at the moment. You are giving up your time, energy, and productivity for social media. Also, you may be giving up your dreams, focus and ambition. Take one day a week to regain all these. It will be worth the sacrifice.

7. Use MIA

This takes us back to the alternatives you have to eliminate. Fewer choices mean more action. Do not let yourself get overloaded with multiple choices because it will definitely slow you down. If you find yourself procrastinating due to too many choices and difficulty making decisions, strategize by visualizing these choices and cutting them down to facilitate decision-making. Once you have decided on your next line of actions, break them down into activities. Then, categorize them into the 3 Most Important Activities (MIA). This list will contain all your to-dos in order of priority.

Then, pick these 3 MIAs you must complete before nightfall once a week. You can add deadlines to these MIAs so that you will have more pressure to deliver at due time. What exactly should be on your MIA list? This depends on you. Think about things you can constantly do that guarantee your long-term success and significant changes. These are activities that concern your health, happiness and dreams. It could be studying, saving, creating, meditating, or anything that significantly impacts your progress and success.

Do not overthink these MIAs. Make them easy and achievable. Do not set unrealistic MIAs. That will make it more difficult and lead to more procrastination and failure in the long run. These MIAs would make it easy for you to track your success and progress. Doing it once a week makes it less of a burden and more effective. If you remain consistent, you may eventually make it a daily activity unconsciously. You can set targets for each MIA to make it more effective. For example, if you have studied on your MIA, you can add the time frame or duration, the number of pages to cover, or the amount of knowledge to gain. Another example is if your target is weight loss, and you have walking on your list, you can add a target of how many steps.

MIAs with targets and time frames make tracking and measuring your success easy. They may be extracurricular but make sure that they contribute to you as a person in a positive way. Don't get scared. Once a week is not too much to achieve. You just need to stay determined and motivated.

8. Take Advantage of Rolling to-do lists.

Another thing that makes us procrastinate is the complexity and difficulty level of the task in question. Just because we get confused about where to start, we keep postponing and thinking we will get it done when the time is right. The truth is, most times, we just keep postponing until the deadline, and then we give up on doing whatever to get the job done. Meanwhile, if we had developed a means to hit the complex task with actions, it would have been a better experience. Avoid this difficult situation daily with a rolling to-do list.

A rolling to-do list is simply a to-do list with more flexibility, perspective and unique time. To get started, break the task into small actions and spread them out appropriately over time. It is just a simple list, but it significantly impacts your productivity. Start by creating a list that contains everything you want to put on your to-do list. This is your master list that includes all your header tasks. Next, break down these header tasks into action items that are smaller, more precise, and more actionable. Try your best to ensure that they are not too much or repetitive. You only try to simplify your tasks, not make a million others. Yes, it may be longer than your typical to-do list but don't panic. These extra steps indicated have always been there but not acknowledged. After making the long list, assign the actionable steps you will tackle the next day. You can pick any task, and following the sequence is not compulsory.

Unlike a master list, this rolling to-do list gives you room for life because you can take one task a day and even roll over an incomplete task to the following day. It can be addictive and motivating as it makes Herculean task become more approachable. You don't have to worry so much about controlling things. Just roll them over. But, this technique is not advisable if you know that you might slack easily. Once a week, every time you define your list of activities, ensure the first activity of the day is identical to the last activity you worked on the previous day. You can leave a task halfway, so it rolls into another day. Before you know it, you gradually roll through the problematic task without overthinking or breaking a nerve in the brain.

9. Hard Things First

After itemizing the list of activities needed to complete a task, we often have this difficult one that keeps us aback. It may not necessarily be tricky, but it requires some rigorous or uncomfortable process and may be something that can take you out of your zone for a while. Activities like this are usually prone to postponing until every other thing has been completed. Well, that could be a wrong choice. Always start with strenuous activities. It is an excellent time management technique and can be a great tool for combatting procrastination. Whether studying a chapter, completing that damn report, or making an important phone call, anything that seems to need some extra work must be the first activity you do every day. It makes you more relaxed to do other things.

In a case where the strenuous activity is a prerequisite to another one on the list, doing it first is a necessity. If you save it for later, you will spend too much time as expected on that single task. You also create room for procrastinating, which can delay the whole project for a more extended period. These complex activities can stand as a blocker to your day. Swallow the toad in the early hours of the day so that you can feel delighted by the progress. Once the task is completed, you get motivated to do smaller ones faster and be free for the day.

Don't let complex activities linger on. The rolling to-do list can also re-surface here to help you take out complex tasks. You can deliberately begin a day before so that you can complete it in the early hours of the next day. This is more than a once-a-week technique and must be your approach to any inappropriate activity that comes your way. For more complicated tasks and large projects, you should have them split in the structure like the WBS. This will help you combat them better. Never neglect a task because of its difficulty. You will still have to face its reality in the future. Taking the bull on its own is not an activity for later. Do it while your brain is still refreshed and your muscle energized.

10. Don't make a mountain out of a pebble.

This is the last tip, and it crowns it all. If you are thinking of all things listed above without acting. You will only make them seem like a huge task. You have made this exercise of fighting procrastination a commitment, and it's time to stop thinking and start acting. Every day you think and don't act, the commitment grows bigger, and it will become impossible to face gradually. Don't make any project seem like a big deal by overthinking it. Get your jigger and start work. Make essential planning and take action accordingly. For instance, you want to lose weight. Instead of thinking about the effect of exercising on your body, how you may not have time for exercising, the difficulties in dieting, and so on. Take the step and start exercising. Create a meal plan that works and get to it.

Sometimes you don't even need to plan. You know exactly what to do, so stop spinning gears in your brain and start doing what should be done. Thinking is not an action. It is exhausting and can cause fatigue. Get your body to act. If you have given it a thought to start the Once-a-week technique, do it without further hesitation. Challenges will come along the way. There is no success without obstacles but don't make a big deal from the beginning. You don't eat by thing about food. There is an obvious process of buying or cooking the meal and eating it.

Your goals should be your focus. That Is the mountain you must climb. Don't make the climbing process another hill. If you need to stop your distractions, avoid them with recommended techniques. Stay true to your commitment so that you can grow. Don't try to give up too much at a time. It should be a process.

These 10 tips above are not just words but actions. If you have read and followed this book to this point, then I am convinced that you have freed yourself from being a slave to procrastination. Having introduced the once-a-week technique, you need to understand how to create the structure that works. I used to be a chronic procrastinator, and these are most of the methods I used in combatting the procrastinating disease.

Chapter 9
Reschedule Your Time One Day a Week

As discussed earlier, you know you can't overcome procrastination at a go, once. That's why you should take things one at a time. Just like Rome was not built in a day, a procrastination-free life cannot be achieved it n a day. It takes consistency and patience to achieve it. You need to know the habits that will help you eliminate procrastination and what you ought to do and the tasks that ought to be completed at a given time. You need to develop habits that will keep you away from those things that get your time stolen. Or even some changes you should make in your health, work, body, and life generally.

So we've made it easy for you, so you won't give up on becoming better by introducing the 'once a week' plan to you.

There are seven days a week and a day is made up of three parts: morning, afternoon, and evening. Based on people's different habits, they will be more or less different. But generally, the three parts can be identified.

You can choose a part of the day (like Monday afternoon, Wednesday morning, or Friday evening) to do one or two of your written down liberating activities, which may be an exercise for those that want their weight reduced, reading for those who have exams, writing for someone who has one or two proposals to submit.

What do you gain from engaging in a habit just to beat procrastination?

Procrastination is a fierce enemy. If you have ever tried to beat it, you'd know that it doesn't leave voluntarily. You have to fight it. Regardless of how difficult it is, if you're struggling with it, you have to push and persevere until you eliminate it. So your efforts are worth it.

The more you resist procrastination and withstand the assaults that come with it, the more you enjoy the benefits embedded in a procrastination-free life. Below are some benefits.

- Your self-control increases: One of the things procrastination does to one is to get you convinced that it is only when you feel like working that you should work. But that will only keep you at the same point. There won't be any moving forward. If you want to achieve great goals, you must learn to work even when you don't feel like it. When you do that, you have great control over yourself. So the more you engage in habits that keep you away from procrastination, the more the control you have over yourself increases.
- Problems are prevented from amplifying: 'Deal with the kitten before it turns into a lion". That's what someone once said. Some problems are so small. They are like a small tear in a cloth. But when you allow procrastination and start delaying dealing with them, they grow in size and experience greatness until they become crises. So it's good you take a bull by the horn. Tackle every problem head-on, so they don't become unsolvable.
- More goals will be achieved: Do you have so many goals you want to achieve by procrastination has been a stumbling block? That's its work. Every time you want to start, it'll come up and hold your hands tight with distractions.
- There are many things you could have started but couldn't because of this great enemy.

When you have great goals and objectives to achieve, procrastination has a way of showing itself. But when you eventually get freed from it, your progress towards your goal will be in strides. This is because how soon you launch determines how soon you will cross the finish line.

- Trustworthiness is shown: Saying you will do something and then procrastinating makes people lose the trust they have for you. Think of those times you've given people assignments but weren't able to deliver at the right time because they procrastinated. You did some yourself, right?

  Overcoming procrastination will make you a better person. You'll always do what you say (that is, you'll always keep your word) and build trust.

- Regrets are avoided: Regret is always coming at the end of every action of procrastination. Perhaps, you allowed distraction and procrastination at a point, regret will come, and you'll start saying, "I shouldn't have...", I could have..." and so on.

  You'll surely regret not being able to pursue your dreams, goals, and potential and showing more self-discipline at points you were supposed to.

  But this is it; when procrastination is present, nothing great can be achieved. You just have to push forth and not allow it.

  Although it pretends to be or act like it is, procrastination never has and never will be on anyone's side. Its main work is trying to get one's goals, dreams, potential, purpose, opportunities, and life stolen. This especially is what makes your habit to overcome it a worthwhile or essential one.

- Opportunities missed are fewer: It's this simple, procrastinating makes you lose opportunities. Yes. Some opportunities don't last; if you don't make use of them 'now' (at the right time), you lose them.

It is a procrastination pleasure to see you indecisive every time. It is well aware of the fact that if you remain indecisive for a long time, you won't be the one to make the decision yourself anymore. It will be made for you. And, of course, it won't be in your favor.

When you work and allow yourself to be free from procrastination, you will always react on time to opportunities that support your vision and values. And you will get them seized.

- More of your potentials are tapped into: True. You tap into more of your potential when you break the arms of procrastination. Procrastination gets your potential stiffened. You tap into your potential when your goals are pursued, and you do great work. Your potentials demand that you do your best possible. It demands that you are responsible, resourceful, and creative. Interestingly, procrastination is against you tapping into them. It says into your inner ears, "it's too difficult; it can't be done now; it's too painful. Do something more interesting like seeing movies."

  You can do it. More than you do, but procrastination which you've not overcome, won't allow, so you settle for less, making your potential lay dormant inside you. And that's a big-time tragedy which is not only to you but to the world at large. For instance, you have so much more to do and offer the world, but because you're still a captive of the enemy- procrastination, your potential won't come alive. They won't see the light of the day or even serve those they were meant to serve.

- There will be an improvement in your work quality: The quality of your work experiences improves when you are not always in rush hour. Overcoming procrastination makes you do better professionally. For instance, if you fail to check the financial result of your company, you know there will be an emergency company-wide.

Basics of the Once-A-Week Plan

- It is an ongoing process: Getting things done like this is similar to going to the gym. If you fail to work on your productivity skills, you've automatically failed to be productive, and procrastination will be the order of the day in your life. Therefore, you have to be accountable and fix your mind and heart on proven strategies like the once-a-week plan below to beat procrastination and move forward.
- You have to enjoy the process: It is very wrong to put your mind on the end goal- the result. It's a straight way to depression. Life does not happen in the future. It happens in the present. So if you are a person who focuses on the future, you are not in the present. So always remember that you must enjoy today. If today is not good enough, make it better. Do not keep hoping that your tomorrow will be better. It is possible you might not be here anymore.
- Nothing is standing alone: Everything is connected to each other. Do you want to beat procrastination? Do you want to get the tasks done? They are both connected to your life, to everything about you: how you view life, how much you sleep, where you go, how seriously you take work, orders you obey, how much you eat, who you spend your time with and so on. This is the main reason tactics don't function well. You must have a holistic strategy in order to live a productive life.
- It improves self-confidence: This is one of the biggest lessons.

You feel better about yourself when you promise yourself to do something, and you get it done. You will be a more reliable person. A person who can execute. This gives you a track record. It also means that you are someone who has the ability to achieve something. Not everyone can say that. So you know, getting procrastination eliminated boosts your self-confidence.

- Embracing accountability births consistency: This can occur in various ways or forms. You can publicly announce your plan or determination to follow the once-a-week plan. You can tell your friends and families about it. But don't think you will be held accountable by people who are not motivated. There are times you've started new activities with close relatives or friends who gave up after a few days or weeks. Do not rely on them. Take your life and career very seriously and find people who have the corresponding mindset.
- You have to learn how to be more effective: You have to know that productivity is a skill that can never be left out of a life that will be meaningful. Not only that. You have to get it sharpened at all times. If not, you will find yourself procrastinating like someone who thinks life has no end. You need to know how to get the most out of your time. You need to be more effective.
- You should get your time protected: Never allow things that are not of any importance. Learn how to say 'no' to some things. Things that are not supposed to be. Learn how to say 'no' to some requests. In a bid to be seen as a good person by everyone, you can't afford to lose your life. Saying yes to everything is a recipe for a meaningless and miserable life. Learn to say 'no' to unimportant things every day. You need not be a party popper. It's simple - be more mindful of your time.
- You will get better each week: Overcoming procrastination takes time. And it is only the consistent that can really do it. But most people are not consistent. That's why many start this plan but don't become successful, overcoming procrastination.

You must be patient. You don't become an achiever in just a day. Like making money with investment, knowledge compounds within years, not days.

- Knowledge work needs a lot of energy: In the economy of today, we need to think outside of the box to get jobs done. Jobs are experiencing more complexity, and we, in turn, need multiple skills for better performance. They require a whole lot of thinking. And thinking is just as hard as physical work. But they aren't treated that way. Make sure your brain is not too strained.
- Everything can be made easier, but that still has to be done: You have to do it. It's a must. Saying you will become better someday is not worth it. It is worthless. That's how it is for earning more money, getting in shape, getting your job done, or even getting a new job. This is the foundation of all kinds of achievement - ACTION.

With great consistency, when you eliminate procrastination and achieve results, you don't have to prove yourself with words any longer. You don't need to explain yourself to people again. It's your result that will do the speaking and explanation. That's the strength of overcoming procrastination. You don't want to get the work done; you want to run from it. Many people do that, but you decided to take a different route, way, or path. Wake up, do the work today, now, do it again the next day, and so on.

So what are we saying? Do all you can to eliminate procrastination. There are a lot of benefits in doing that, just as there is a lot of harm that will be done if it remains.

The liberating activities in the previous chapter can serve as open doors to liberation from procrastination. They can be used to create a habit that will turn our faces or turn us from procrastination.

Dedicate a part of the day to one or two of the ten liberating activities mentioned in the chapter before.

For instance:

Monday morning - Use MIA. Starting with your to-do list, eliminate excess choices. You know, when there are too many choices, you'll remain indecisive for a long time. This time of the day, bring out your to-do list and bring out three MIAs which stand for the Most Important Activities you intend to complete before that time. Activities like these may be those that can have a great impact on your life even till the next five years. They generally have to do with your happiness, health, and secret dreams.

So on Monday mornings, for as many weeks as you want to practice this same habit, know that you have to use the MIAs. Even if you don't have tasks that will affect you in the next five years, you can choose those that will affect your entire week, or even the day at least. - The most important tasks. For instance, you can decide to wash and iron the clothes you'd be putting on for the rest of the week or even the week's food timetable.

Tuesday afternoon - Media diet. This is a great distraction that contributes to our tendency to procrastinate. Among all the distractions that exist, media and technological distractions generally are the most common that many people struggle with. That is, technological distractions have more victims than the rest.

If you are too addicted to it that it takes most of your time, you can decide to observe media fast or media diet every Tuesday afternoon for as many weeks as possible. Give up Instagram, WhatsApp, Facebook, Twitter, and other social networks. Do away with TV programs of dubious value and online news.

So as not to forget, you can set a reminder on your phone or write and paste it in a place you'll always see it and get reminded.

If you think the media diet is too much for you to do, think of how many of your dreams you have been giving up and those you are likely to give up if you don't thread this path of correction.

So every Tuesday afternoon, you aren't with anything called media.

Wednesday evening - Moment of idleness. Make your Wednesday evenings your moment of idleness. Although you can still move forward by having your moment of idleness every day, you can start with this at first. At times, procrastinating intentionally can have effects that are beneficial. With a minimum and maximum of 15 and 60 minutes, respectively. So dedicate this part or period of your Wednesdays to activities that keep you charged or that recharge you. Those activities include meditating, sports, reading, and so on, etc.

For instance, if you've done one thing or the other since the beginning of the day, you are expected or advised to create a time or moment of idleness. Maybe you've been writing proposals upon proposals since morning, or you've been engaged in anything intellectual; you could go out for fresh air in the evening and listen to music while taking a nice ice cream with very awesome taste.

Or you've been washing since you woke up or doing other house chores; you can create a moment of idleness in the evening by watching sports, meditating, or reading.

So note that every evening on Wednesdays is for your moment of idleness. And since you know that, you should also know that you won't be able to observe it if you've not been busy since the beginning of that day. Or does it make any sense to observe a moment of idleness when in actual sense, you've been idle since you woke up that day.

Thursday afternoon - Make use of creative visualization. What does it mean? It means imagining yourself reaching your goals or accomplishing all that you have been aspiring to accomplish. What you'd do and how you'd feel. This is a motivation, in addition to action, which is birthed from the right perception of reality.

It may be for ten (10) minutes every Thursday afternoon; just imagine yourself reaching your goals.

This liberating activity has great effectiveness. But its effectiveness can only be visible if you are focused on the process and your feelings about achieving your aims, goals, and objectives.

Set your reminder, and don't miss this activity every Thursday afternoon. It helps you to know or have a taste of how much happiness you will have after accomplishing your set goals. It draws your heart doing them, and you'll see that your commitment to them increases.

Friday morning - Do the hard things first. Consider that every Friday morning. Although this technique is not perfect for managing time, it's still a very good weapon for fighting against procrastination.

Be it visiting a friend (as a person who doesn't like going out), studying for exams, writing a report, washing a heap of clothes, making that important phone call, writing or checking the proposals, or buying the needed foodstuff at home, or writing the project, do it now. Tackle it now - this Friday morning.

Don't have the mind or allow the thought of "it's a Friday, Monday should be for things like these- important things like this" No! Don't do that. It's actually procrastination raising its ugly head. So don't allow it.

Doing the difficult tasks first and making headway with them gives you the joy that you ride on throughout the day. It even makes it easier for you to do other things remaining, more than you even expect or thought of doing. You know, joy is a great strength on its own.

So, every Friday morning, do the difficult things first.

Saturday evening - Act, despite everything. It's not every time you feel like doing something. But do not let that thought linger in your heart because your heart has a way of controlling all that has to do with you. It is the seat of your life. Or, let's say, the steering wheel. So your life always follows its direction (the direction of your heart).

Someone once said that once you allow the thought of "I am tired" to linger in your heart, you will become really tired, too tired to do that which you ought to do. Even if you are not really tired, you will become tired because your heart has decided to believe that.

So act despite everything. Do not even try to wait till you are ready like you always say to yourself -"I don't think I'm ready. When I'm ready, I will do a perfect job; it won't even take long". Don't do that. Don't wait till you are ready or even confident. If you do, you may never reach that goal because that time may never come.

So every Saturday evening, try to do a task that you are not comfortable with. That is not convenient for you, one that you would prefer to postpone to a better time.

Sunday afternoon - Use this time to take advantage of a rolling to-do list. Yes, that should be done once a week. What does this mean? Ensuring that the first activity you do today has a connection to the last one you did yesterday.

One of the reasons we find ourselves unable to tackle complex projects that we keep postponing and postponing is that we don't know where to start.

So for you not to continue being in that situation, you are advised to take advantage of the rolling to-do list once a week, ensuring the first thing you do on Sunday is the last thing you did on Saturday. In other words, define your list of activities in a way that your first activity in a day is identical to the last activity you were working on the day before.

Sometimes, you can intentionally leave the work half done on Saturday to continue on from there on Sunday.

That helps too.

Chapter 10

THE ROAD TO FREEDOM. ONCE A WEEK, NOT ONCE.

What is freedom itself?

Freedom is what many people dream about, speak about, think about, and even celebrate. It is what many advocate and hope for. But what does it mean?

It is of different meaning to many people. To some, it can mean having the chance to vote or stand for certain ideas or people who can represent their views best. To some, it can be seen from the perspective of freedom of speech, being able to voice out personal perspectives or opinions without any hindrance. Others may see it from a financial perspective, where they seek to get freed from burdensome loans, financial debts, and outstanding credit.

But what is the picture of true freedom?

Is it someone getting out of prison? Is it the ballot of a voter? Is it the ability or opportunity to do anything a person wants or the ability to owe anything to anyone?

According to Merriam-Webster, freedom is the quality or state of being free. Like the absence of coercion, necessity, or constraints in action or choice; like being liberated from slavery, oppression, or the power of another. Like boldness of execution or conception or a political right. It can also be deliverance from addiction.

It is more complicated than the ability to do whatever we want to do. In truth, freedom can be the right to think, speak, gather, do, believe, worship, or act as one like. But it is so only until a person's choices start to infringe on someone else's freedom.

It can be defined as a state of mind where you have the ability, chance, or opportunity to do what you can think of without any restriction. You can feel freedom from within you.

Only those who have earned something, experienced it, or even sacrificed something big, can know its real value. You can't really know the value of being free from procrastination if you are not free. But there's no doubt you will experience its great harm in full force.

If you are a procrastinator, I'm sure you have always wanted to be free from it. You always have or sometimes want it to stop so you can be better or live a better life. You've even probably asked yourself this question-

"Why do I keep procrastinating even though I know it is bad for me? And even though I want to stop?" Why do you think you still procrastinate? **Why is it so difficult to be free from it?**

It is the assumption of many people that their procrastination is a result of the absence of willpower or even laziness. But that's not true, really. The actual answer is much more complex than that. It has to do with the cognitive mechanisms that we use to regulate our behavior, in our wanting to bring ourselves to take action that is best for us.

In summary, when we need to do a specific thing, we always depend on our self-discipline or self-control to get ourselves to do it. Also, our motivation which is determined by the desire for some reward that we will get as a result of completing that task can provide a boost that is helpful to our ability to control or discipline ourselves, which in turn helps us to act timely.

However, there are varieties of demotivating factors, which include anxiety or fear of failure, that have a negative effect on our motivation. This implies that they can make us more likely to get out tasks postponed unnecessarily instead of getting them done at the right time.

Also, there are various factors that work as a hindrance. They include distracting environments and rental exhaustion that disturbs our ability to control ourselves and our motivation directly in a way that also makes us more likely to procrastinate.

Whenever these factors (the hindering factors and the demotivating ones) are greater than our motivation and self-control, we end up procrastinating even when we don't want to. We just will not be able to help it. We now have to give time for the balance between them to shift back to favour us before we can do the work. This can take very long sometimes.

For every feeling you have, your brain releases a corresponding chemical. More feelings birth more similar chemicals. The procrastination cycle can take you through numerous feelings which may not be necessarily negative. Procrastination as an act gives a sense of immediate gratification. Think about how you feel when you get off the hook and decide to 'do it later.'

You are aware you have a deadline, it's really on your mind, but immediately you tell yourself you'll do it later; you experience a feeling of relief which is a kind of chemical response. So to get the cycle perpetuated, you create bigger ways to get more feelings of relief. You just have to get the ante up.

You might have experienced the exhilaration of making a deadline narrowly. You might have felt excited then. But that doesn't excuse procrastination of the negative feelings like dread, fear, guilt, embarrassment (etc) that come with it so often. Whatever feelings you have again and again will give the same chemical reaction in your system.

At last, you become dependent on those feelings that birth the chemicals you now rest on. The same way a person craves nicotine and caffeine is the same way your body now craves the chemicals your brain produced based on whatever you have created habitually.

However, by using the once-a-week technique, which you will find in this chapter, it is possible to shift the balance in your favour without much stress in a short time. This will allow you to control your life and give you the ability to get your tasks done when you want to and not when your procrastination allows you to.

The Road to Freedom

The road to freedom is the path to hope for you who want procrastination eliminated from your life. Those who are in pain caused by procrastination, or even those who are simply stuck in it. Are you one of those who start a journey only to return without getting to the destination? If yes, procrastination really has the upper hand over you. If it is a road, you don't just take a step and get tired or stop. You are expected to walk down the road till the end.

Do you want to walk down the lane or path that overcomes procrastination, but you get tired along the way? No! That shouldn't be. If you've started the liberating habit once a week, don't get tired. Don't stop. It is once a week; it isn't once. So you shouldn't stop after trying it once. That will lead you nowhere. It is just as good as not doing it at all. So try all your best possible to see that you stick to that plan.

Fine, it isn't easy. But whenever you feel tired and want to stop, just think of the great harm procrastination has been doing in your life. Think of the benefits embedded in overcoming it.

Overcoming procrastination is a process that cannot be finished at once. Begin the process of recovery by going about the once-a-week plan in the chapter before. You will find answers there. It even teaches you how great small and steady improvement is, compared to an overnight change. So face your problem, face the procrastination eating you up, and focus on the road to freedom. That's the only way to heal and become better. Failure to do that is failure to accept freedom.

12 Quotes on Road to Freedom

1. "*People don't realise that to be free means to be firmly attached to a system, that discipline is the road to a higher freedom*" - Author: Chandrasekharendra Saraswati.

   It isn't easy, but you have to discipline yourself. You know, not doing it will do great harm with no good at all. So you just have to deny yourself of the temporary pleasure it gives and be determined to don't. You can even let others close to you know about the plan, so when you are derailing from it, they will get you cautioned.

2. "*The road to freedom is a difficult, hard road. It always makes for temporary setbacks*" - Martin Luther King Jr.

It's a difficult, hard road, but he who wants freedom at all costs will do it.

3. *The best road to progress is freedom's road.* - Author: John F. Kennedy

   The once-a-week plan is freedom's road itself. As you follow, you'll see yourself always thinking of the plan, and this will make it possible for you to focus on becoming better.

4. *The road to freedom is full of thorns and fire, yet happy is he who follows it!* - Author: Aminu Kano

Yes, in the end, it is happiness. The result is happiness. As someone who procrastinates, I know you will be familiar with that feeling of guilt, depression, and unhappiness that fills your mind when you fail to do something you ought to do or accomplish your task.

So following the once-a-week plan till the end, not just trying it once, will take those negative feelings away from you.

5. *The road to freedom is a beautiful system* - Author: Phil Jackson

   The once-a-week plan is a beautiful system. By itself, it attracts you to itself.

6. *Freedom is a heavy load, a great and strange burden for the spirit to undertake. It is not easy. It is not a gift given but a choice made, and the choice may be a hard one. The road goes upward towards the light; but the laden traveler may never reach the end of it.* - Author: Ursula K. Le Guin

   You have the choices before you- embarking on the road to freedom (once-a-week plan) or continuing on the dangerous path of procrastination.
   You may feel you don't want to get yourself stressed or make yourself inconvenient, but making that choice that's difficult

to make, the one that doesn't give the present sweetness, is the better choice.

7. *The road to freedom lies, not through mysteries or occult performances, but through the intelligent use of Nature's forces and laws. The Law of Mind is a natural law in the spiritual world.* - Author: Ernest Holmes

   Start the plan from your mind. Let the long-lasting benefits dominate your mind. Convince your mind to know that that's the road to freedom, and you can't afford to lose it. When the mind knows this, you follow it without much stress.

8. *Self-reliance is the only road to true freedom, and being one's own person is its ultimate reward* - Author: Patricia Sampson

   Be sure of yourself. Believe in yourself. You can do it. You can take your ownership of procrastination and own it yourself.

9. *I climb behind the steering wheel... I drive off immediately without once looking back; it's a long journey but it leads to freedom.* - Author: Corinne Hofmann

   Sometimes, you just have to take your eyes off how much distance you've covered. If not, you may either become discouraged or relaxed. For instance, if you see you've made much progress, you'll feel relaxed - "Oh! I didn't know I've covered as much as this". But if the opposite is the case, you may become very discouraged and want to stop - " I just know I can't do it. It's just not for me." So you should try not to even take a look at the back till you are sure you won't stop no matter what.

10. *You can't stop us on the road to freedom, you can't stop us cause our eyes can see.* - Author: Van Morrison

    Don't stop. Let nothing stop you from moving forward. Do not allow distractions because you can see the good in it on the road.

11. *A policy of freedom for the individual is the only truly progressive policy.* - Author: Friedrich August Von Hayek

Take the once-a-week plan as your own personal plan. That's only when there will be progress.

12. *Obedience is the road to freedom.* - Author: C.S. Lewis

Obey the once-a-week plan as much as possible. Follow it strictly, and you'll find yourself moving forward on the road to freedom, almost reaching it.
If you have already made the once-a-week plan a habit. Congratulation to you. But you know you can improve, right? You can. When you notice you are used to the plan in the previous chapter, you can add other liberating activities. Let's take a look at this.

This is the first one:

Monday	**M**orning	Use MIA.
Tuesday	**A**fternoon	Media diet.
Wednesday	**E**vening	Moment of idleness
Thursday	**A**fternoon	Make use of creative visualization.
Friday	**M**orning	Do the hard things first.
Saturday	**E**vening	Act, despite everything.
Sunday	**A**fternoon	Use this time to take advantage of a rolling to-do list.

The above is the first one. You can practice that for a minimum of three weeks. Then, you can add one more liberating activity to each day. You can do the new ones in another period of the day. So altogether, you'll be doing two liberation activities in a day.

DAY	**PERIOD**	**LIBERATING ACTIVITIES**
Monday	Morning Evening	Use MIA - Most Important Activities Magic phrase
Tuesday	Afternoon Evening	Media diet Avoid the trap of result
Wednesday	Morning Evening	Don't make a mountain out of pebbles Moment of idleness
Thursday	Morning Afternoon	Act despite everything* Make use of creative virtualization
Friday	Morning Afternoon	Do the hard things first. Magic phrase*
Saturday	Afternoon Evening	*Avoid the trap of result Act despite everything
Sunday	Morning Afternoon	Use MIA* Take advantage of the rolling to-do list

Most of the liberation activities have been explained. Let's explain the remaining three.

Magic phrase: One of the things you should know is that there are only two things in this life. They are excuses and results. If you allow excuses, be sure you are not going to get the result expected of the work.

Whenever you find yourself repeating phrases or accommodating their thoughts in your heart, "I don't feel like doing it now; after all, it's not that serious or important; I work better under pressure," all you have to do is to put down the date and time and the magic phrase in a book that is special, that you won't lose easily.

So you know, Monday evening is for magic phrase.

Avoid the trap of results: There are times you have wanted everything right away, right? You wanted the result to be all you are and have been doing, right?

Let me tell you the truth. If you continue doing that, you won't see yourself moving forward and you will always get discouraged from continuing.

Now is the time to adopt a habit that will help you avoid the trap of results. So for one day in a week, and four or five times in a month, do not have anything to do with judgement on results.

For instance, rise up in the morning and follow your diet without paying attention to the results you are getting. Or start working out and not check if it's having effects or not.

The only thing you need to watch for is your progress. You can do that by making use of a chain or climbing. But you don't have to care about the results.

Remember, Tuesday evening is for avoiding the trap of results.

Don't make a mountain out of pebbles: A commitment only becomes magnified if the only thing you do about it is think and not face it. Every time you do this, that task grows bigger and bigger until it becomes difficult or even impossible to face. Make important planning and act rightly.

Planning is not even necessary sometimes, especially when you know what you have to do. So don't get the gears of your brain spinning, and start 'NOW.'

Your liberating activity for every Wednesday morning is - Don't make a mountain out of a pebble.

What happens when you keep procrastinating?

At the very beginning, the effect of procrastination may not seem bad at all, but over time, it can build and result in anxiety, low self-esteem, stress, and broken dreams. Instead of allowing procrastination to relax in you, why not take time to develop time management techniques that will help you deal with it when it comes to raising its ugly head?

Some people might be fortunate to recognize their tendency to procrastinate and do something about it, but others might not be so lucky. And it can end up affecting them for a long which may resonate all through their lives.

The reason people procrastinate might vary from one person to another. And it's not always visible or obvious. Sometimes it is the fear of failure which we don't want to admit; we don't just want to do it because we aren't motivated to do it.

No matter the reason, a procrastinator must be careful because he is prone to many damaging effects that he may not even know.

Below are the consequences of not overcoming procrastination:

- Losing opportunities: Procrastination will make you waste many opportunities because you failed to take advantage of them when they were still present. You didn't realize that the opportunity could be a door to a change of life and you missed out on it. Opportunities like that only come once. They may never come again. Opportunities are the ways the world gives you more so you can help yourself and grab them well immediately they get to you, or you see them.
- Ruining career: The way you work directly affects your result and how well you perform and achieve, so procrastination can end up putting your career at stake. It may hinder you from meeting deadlines and targets. You know what that means.

  There are chances or possibilities you will miss out on a promotion meant for you or even be at risk of losing your job. You can do well trying to hide it for some time. But there's certainly no doubt that long-term procrastination at work can ruin your career.

- Poor decisions: This is one of the worst effects of procrastination. It makes you make decisions according to criteria that may not be there if you didn't allow procrastination, such as pressure to decide on something because time is almost up. Our emotions greatly affect the decisions we make; you are aware that procrastination is good at increasing negative emotions. This can cause you to make decisions that won't serve you for long.

  Why rush through decisions while procrastinating when you can own down all the possibilities and calmly find a moment to do the analysis of the pros and cons of each one of them?

- Health risks: Another effect of procrastination is mental health problems which include anxiety and stress. These are, in turn, linked to health issues. If procrastination causes you to be depressed, be sure it will start affecting other areas of your life.

If you allow procrastination a lot with something, there is a high possibility you will get stressed out anxiety will come in, especially when other factors like things and people are involved. All these can lead to poor health outcomes.

There is another way procrastination can have a negative effect on your health when you put off check-ups continually and get appointments or things to be done like postponing exercise.

- Losing precious time: Do you know how much time you have wasted procrastinating again and again? The bad thing about it is the moment you realize how much time has gone and you've not really done anything meaningful, or nothing has changed. There's this terrible feeling that comes just because you can't reverse the time. You know you have no other choice than to live with that terrible feeling, knowing the situation could not have been like that if you hadn't procrastinated, if only you had taken the step.
- Damage to reputation: You making promises and ending up not fufiling them can get your image tarnished, as no one wants empty promises. No one wants to risk their job or career to give you assignments. Apart from getting your reputation damaged, your self-esteem is also at risk. You won't find it difficult to procrastinate anymore because you don't surprise yourself again.

People could stop relying on you. They will hold back on offering you opportunities because they know you might procrastinate, and they end up cleaning the mess.

Even if people already know you as a procrastinator, you can change your image so that next time someone asks you for something, you will make use of all your tools to get it done in time. Each time you do that, your reputation will begin to build again. This will open the door for more opportunities for you. There is also a greater chance for better relationships with those around you.

Conclusion

It Worked Once. Why Couldn't It Work Again? Overcoming procrastinating requires hard work. It's not easy at all. It takes consistent applied effort and energy and focuses on being free from old patterns of behaviours that have been holding you back from being your very best for all this time.

Of course, you have great potentials that have not been tapped into at all and the ability to be and achieve all your heart desires. You have been holding yourself back for so long. You have been denying yourself the opportunities to get your goals accomplished. But not anymore. You are now a different person. Your sense of energy and confidence is now renewed. That will drive you forward toward better and bigger things. Not even procrastination will dare to stand in your way.

Yes, if you've tried the once-a-week plan, or if I've tried it once and it worked, why couldn't it work again? Of course, it can. It could work again. The primary key is just patience and consistency. And just like we've said before, don't fix your eyes and mind on the result. Take your mind off it for some time or the once-a-week you have set. In the nearest future, you will see yourself becoming better.

It is very important to take steps to eliminate resistance and then give your best effort to stop it. However, in order to overcome this chronic trap called procrastination, you need to be consistent with the once-a-week plan to get started with a positive habit. When triggers, that is, things that prompt you to perform those habits in the plan, like the place, time of the day, and circumstances are the same, it is easier to stick.

In whatever way, our habits have a way of defining us. The good ones can lead us to be progressive and successful. At the same time, the bad ones can cause us to fail. So consistently performing the good ones means being dedicated to your goals and staying focused on those things and activities to achieve your goals. Consistency requires a long-term commitment from you. It also involves sustained effort in repeatedly following the tabled plan in this book until you have achieved your goals.

Consistency is not easy, but you have to be disciplined. Discipline yourself to be to free yourself from your enemy - procrastination. Below are some of the ways you can keep yourself consistent with the plan:

Place reminders around your workplace, home, or belongings: It is normal to forget our daily routines, especially when we are new to them. Always remember, you are advised to put messages to yourself in visible areas.

Reward yourself when you get something done: Give yourself a reward whenever you complete your goals or plan for a day. No matter how small the goals are, reward yourself after completing them. This will keep you motivated throughout the process. For instance, if you complete your plan for Tuesday, You can give yourself a treat.

Keep going even if you make a mistake: There is no perfect person anywhere. Even the most organized and consistent people make mistakes at times. That's why you shouldn't be depressed when you sometimes slip up—plan for future failures. Just because you had to skip a habit does not make you inconsistent. Sometimes, external factors can get in our way despite our planning and preparedness.

Use motivational tools to keep going even when you don't feel like it: It can be easy to overlook your goals for a day when you're stressed or tired, but doing that can quickly cause you to get off track. Whenever you feel this way, just try to find new sources of motivation. You can do this by reminding yourself of your long-term goals. Say to yourself, "if I want to achieve these goals, I will have to get this task done, or I will have to follow the plan."

Give time to notice changes: Note that the OaW plan can take time. Instead of doing many things at once, just be patient with yourself. Usually, it takes three weeks of consistency to make a new habit. Don't rush yourself. Wait until three to four weeks before effecting changes to the plan before adding new habits, which should not be too many. Don't tackle too many.

Build your willpower: To achieve your aim, your willpower must not be weak. Avoid temptation wherever possible. For instance, if you want to follow the plan, ensure you don't have things that will oppose it. Don't have options or alternatives that will take your time and hinder you from following the plan. Another thing that can weaken your willpower is exhaustion. Exhaustion can make you skip tasks. So get a good sleep at night to build your willpower. Also, always remind yourself of the long-term benefits you will derive from following the plan whenever you don't feel motivated. You will get inspiration from reading over and over again your list of goals.

Do away with negative thoughts: Negative thoughts reduce your willpower and consistency. When you allow them, you hinder yourself from holding on to the plans. When you notice negative thoughts creeping in, just turn them around and bring in a more positive or neutral one. For instance, if thoughts like "I can't do this" comes, just turn them around into "I am going to practice doing this even though I'm not too good at it." Pay attention to negative thoughts when they come and catch them before they linger.

Now that you understand how to go about the plan and that consistency is one of the major keys, don't wait. Start 'now'. You have all the tools and weapons to fight procrastination and achieve your goals and overcome the mountains you think we're insurmountable.

Face obstacles by reducing macro-problems into micro-problems. Break your big projects into smaller ones. Break them into bits and achieve them one after the other. Don't try to do it at once.

The once-a-week method can change you as a person, not just to overcome procrastination. It is a method of approaching problems and life generally. It is not just a procrastination cure.

What would you think if I told you that a person could do the following:

Become better OaW

Quit smoking OaW

Lose weight OaW

Fight anxiety OaW

Spend more time with your children OaW

Get in shape OaW

Save money OaW

Go vegan OaW

Leave your smartphone alone OaW

The once-a-week method is what you can use to become that picture of yourself that you have created or made in your mind. Start it now. Don't wait till you've lost many opportunities or till many of your potentials are lost. Start it now and watch your life transform positively or takes a positive turn.

Books like this will be produced in the nearest future. Expect new publications on this same topic - procrastination.

If you like the method, lend the book to your friends, siblings, relative, classmates, and others who need it. It'll be of great help to them too.

You know you can't live life alone. You need people too. But if they are not free from procrastination, be sure you will get affected. You won't be successful on things you assign to them. You'll always get disappointed, and there'll be nothing to do about it. You can't hate them or push them away. So, to help them or not to get affected, you have to help them. Lend them the book, and live a procrastination-free life. Build a better life for yourself and others around you.

Made in the USA
Monee, IL
03 March 2023

29044716R00090